T   ITER

Studies in Judaism and Christianity

*Exploration of Issues in the
Contemporary Dialogue Between
Christians and Jews*

Editor in Chief for
Stimulus Books
Helga Croner

Editors
Lawrence Boadt, C.S.P.
Helga Croner
Leon Klenicki
John Koenig
Kevin A. Lynch, C.S.P.

 A STIMULUS BOOK

TOWARD
A THEOLOGICAL ENCOUNTER

Jewish Understandings of Christianity

Leon Klenicki,
editor

A STIMULUS BOOK
PAULIST PRESS ♦ NEW YORK ♦ MAHWAH

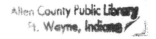
Copyright ©1991 by
Stimulus Foundation

Library of Congress Cataloging-in-Publication Data

Toward a Theological Encounter: Jewish understandings of Christianity/Leon Klenicki, editor.
    p. cm.—(Studies in Judaism and Christianity) (A Stimulus book)
    Includes bibliographical references and index.
    ISBN 0-8091-3256-7
    1. Judaism — Relations — Christianity. 2. Christianity and other religions—Judaism. I. Klenicki, Leon. II. Series.
    BM535.W47   1991
    261.2'6—dc20   91-3305
                                              CIP

Published by Paulist Press
997 Macarthur Boulevard
Mahwah, N.J. 07430

Printed and bound in the United States of America

Contents

Toward a Process of Healing: Understanding the Other as a Person of God

Rabbi Leon Klenicki

> We live in an unredeemed world. But out of each human life that is unarbitrary and bound to the world, a seed of redemption falls into the world, and the harvest is God's.
>
> *Martin Buber*

I see it every time I leave the synagogue. On Saturday morning after services, while going home, it is there, waiting for me, challenging me. It is the cross of a nearby church. Why does it disturb me? The sanctity of the day is marred by an image projecting memories of the past, memories transmitted by generations, by my parents. They are images of contempt for my people. I am overwhelmed despite my own religious feelings of fellowship and my commitment to an ongoing dialogue with Christians. The cross is there, a challenge to my own belief!

I realized that I did not think of the cross as a symbol of Christianity. I was looking at a symbol of a group of people who in the name of their own religion had been unkind, at times evil to my own people. I felt uneasy, ambiguous about the cross. And suddenly came another image. It was of a young woman whom I often see in the subway. She always reads the same little volume, a New Testament. She studies it prayerfully as I do every morning in my own tradition. I empathize with her spirituality, I feel that we share something mysterious, though committed in different ways. Perhaps she might not understand my spirituality, even deny it, but we are together in God.

1

I feel the need to understand the other as a person of God. Can it be done? Can I really be a religious person putting aside a fellow community that is rooted in my own allegiance to God? Can I disregard two thousand years of history, avoiding the representatives of that covenantal relationship? Can I look into the first century and neglect to see God's call to Jesus and the early Christians? Can the pain of history alienate me as it did Christians for centuries? Can I learn to think about Christianity through an encounter with Christians?

HISTORY AND UNDERSTANDING: THE FIRST CENTURY

For centuries, both Jews and Christians have been in disputation, a process fueled by Christian authorities, that resulted in prejudice and self-righteous attitudes. Jews are thought of as objects of faith rather than the I-Thou subjects of a faith relationship. The new challenge of our time is the recognition that we are distinct groups of faith and spirituality who now can meet face to face, acknowledging a common ground of being.

Aware of this reality, the 1974 Vatican *Guidelines and Suggestions for Implementing the Conciliar Declaration "Nostra Aetate"* clearly state the following:

> To tell the truth, such relations as there have been between Jews and Christians have scarcely ever risen above the level of monologue. From now on, real dialogue must be established.
> Dialogue presupposes that each side wishes to know the other, and wishes to increase and deepen its knowledge of the other. It constitutes a particularly suitable means of favoring a better mutual knowledge and, especially in the case of dialogue between Jews and Christians, of probing the riches of one's own tradition. Dialogue demands respect for the other as he is; above all, respect for his faith and his religious convictions.[1]

The Vatican II text needs fulsome consideration, over and over again. The dialogue relationship requires that we acknowledge and committedly reflect on one another. To perceive the other's faith as a call of God is the sine qua non of any meeting. It means that we relate to an existential reality: the other's faith which exists independently of my own thinking. The dialogue relationship accepts the other, the Jewish or Christian person or community, as independent, free, vibrant, unique extensions of God, unfettered by my own ideological or theological projections.

Our dialogue occurs at a specific time in human history, and we are in crisis. I take the word in its *koine* meaning: crisis is a time of turning. Jews and Christians face turning points in their religious thinking and vocations. For the Jewish people as for Judaism, the twentieth century has been a time of death and resurrection. The holocaust is a desolate factor of human cruelty and the diabolic potentialities of the human being. Germany performed the execution, while the crime was in general accepted by the rest of Europe. The Holocaust marks a serious blow to two thousand years of western religious preaching and mission. It reminds all of us that paganism is still a reality and a presence in our midst. Its diabolic nature challenges Jewish witness of God, Christian mission to the world, and particularly the religious obligation of testifying in defense of the human being, God's creation.

One painful aspect of our death experience was the fact that Jews went alone to their final destiny; few voices claimed, protested, such crimes. Is it not a sad reality to the Christian call that in general the community chose silence, when one million children went to the gas chambers? Such lack of words helped the oppressors to act freely and without hindrance.

We have come to know the meaning of an historical resurrection: the state of Israel which was created on the land promised to Abraham. The memory and image of this land is a daily experience in Jewish prayer and ritual. After exile, we now know the redemptive meaning of return. We are at a turning point in our testimony of God; after death, after Auschwitz, we have in return the state of Israel. We are in search, as were Ezra and Nehemiah, of a spirituality of faith in a world invaded by unbelief, easy-going ideologies, and materialism. Once again we are witnessing the eternity of God to a universe of transitory values.

Christians, especially Roman Catholics, are facing a time of crisis, a turning point in their faith commitments as well. *Nostra Aetate,* the Vatican II document on Jews and Judaism, marks a unique moment, a *heshbon ha nefesh,* a reckoning of the soul in search of new meanings and new expressions of religious existence and interpretations of God's command. It is a difficult period in the life of Christians. They have to overcome certain ideas and customs in Christian life that originated in previous eras and must be adapted, after centuries of history and change, to present insights.

Jointly we live in a new time, a turning point in our spiritual commitments. Time is for us, and, we believe, for any deeply concerned person, marked by a "before" and "after," before Auschwitz and after Auschwitz.

For Catholics time is marked by the significant experience of before Vatican II and after Vatican II.

Separately and together we live at a very creative moment in our faiths. We have initiated the dialogue at a time when we are challenged by a prophetic call that will change our spiritual vocations. This relationship obligates us to recognize one another's different spiritual reality and readiness to try to understand the other's faith commitment.

UNDERSTANDING: A PAINFUL PROCESS

Understanding the other is not easy for Jews and Christians because we must surmount two thousand years of prejudice and memory. A hard endeavor indeed! For Christians that involves overcoming triumphalism, recognizing theological and social prejudices that have been and still are present in Christian thinking and actions. Judaism used to be disregarded, fossilized, in theological considerations that denied the eternal validity of the Tanach, the Hebrew Bible, the oral teaching as embodied in rabbinic theology, and the continuing, evolving spiritual growth of Judaism right down to our own days. Prejudice became a violent fact in the days of medieval disputations that ended in the expulsion of entire Jewish communities from cities and countries. Prejudice was reflected in the murderous incursions of the crusaders, massacring and destroying Jews and Jewish communities, on their way to the holy land.

We Jews must surmount two thousand years of memories that haunt us with images of the past, many of them referred to as legends by our parents, the memory of memories. We must overcome the memory of Constantine, of the church fathers' contempt for our tradition, of medieval confrontations, of the ghettos. We must overcome the polite antisemitism of the nineteenth century, the silence that surrounded the Holocaust, the ideological indifference for Israel's struggle for survival. We must overcome also the temptation of self-righteousness! Both Jews and Christians must rid themselves of triumphalism.

Can Christians remodel their approach toward Judaism, setting aside theological pre-conceptions that diminish the significance and role of Israel in God's design? Can Judaism be acknowledged as a faith commitment of its own, an evolving faith that fructifies theological creativity even in our own days? Can the previously mentioned reader on the subway come to realize and accept that the New Testament did not supersede the *Tanach,* which was further developed by the Pharisees and expounded upon by the rabbis and sages?

In overcoming millennia of memories, Jews must face a form of self-righteousness that ignored Christians as part of the people of God. At times suffering has blinded us and we are prone to forget more fortunate periods in our history. We also fear to become too close to Christians. Does better insight into Christianity lead to a change of our testimony and our religious vocation? Is understanding and empathy the first stage of conversion, or do we feel that proximity will lead to syncretism? Why are we so insecure?

There have been Jewish attempts at understanding Christianity in the past. The *Sepher Ikkarim,* Book of Principles, by Joseph Albo, and the *Hizuq Emunah,* Faith Strengthened, by Isaac Troki, are only two such examples. But these approaches were born out of disputations, apologetic pieces defending the main postulates of Judaism that had been challenged by ecclesiastical and theological authorities. Medieval and post-medieval attempts at understanding Christianity related to an *object* of faith, a community that contemptuously attacked Judaism and its right to exist. The recognition by Jews of Christianity as a *subject* of faith is a recent phenomenon, a product of the industrial revolution and, particularly, the North American experience. Jewish theologians have tried, and are trying to this day, to fathom the meaning of Christianity, but there still persists a sense of ambiguity in the interfaith relationship.

THE AMBIGUITY OF A RELATIONSHIP

Ambiguity is part of the Jewish perception of Christianity, i.e. doubtful, open to more than one interpretation, equivocal. These terms define the Jewish approach to Christianity which is closely linked to the experiences of the past. This ambiguity deserves to be reflected upon in light of history, especially the significance of the first century. For a long time I personally found it difficult to call the days of Christianity's beginning the first century. It is a Christian classification rather than a Jewish accounting of time. Yet the study of the origins of rabbinic Judaism and Pharisaism made me realize that the first century was of great importance to both early Christianity and rabbinic Judaism. It also allows me to understand the meaning of our vocations.

The time before and after the destruction of the Jerusalem temple marked a unique moment in Jewish religious thought and the experience of the covenantal relationship. Jewish religious pluralism flourished at that time in a country under the political domination of Rome. Herod's death and the political incompetence of his children who inherited the kingdom initiated a time of social and political unrest, resulting in attacks on Roman troops and in Jewish political struggles. Finally, in the year 6 of the Common Era, Rome decided to make Judea and its related territories into a province. A procurator ruled the country and the high priest of the temple became the religious and political figure responsible to Roman officials. The Roman procurator, however, had final authority. He elected the high priest and kept the sacred Yom Kippur vest in his possession.

Jews had some legal independence in religious matters through the Sanhedrin, the supreme council and tribunal of the second temple. The high priest, by virtue of his office, acted as president, but his opinion in legal religious matters was not seriously considered by the seventy judges of the court, many of them coming from the Pharisaic movement. The Sanhedrin was not an instrument of Rome, as was the high priest, and better represented the Jewish community.

A movement of spiritual renewal had begun with Ezra and Nehemiah in the fourth century B.C.E. It was a process of clarification and interpretation that would engage teachers and scribes for several centuries. Interpretation inevitably involves a reshaping of the text to make it meaningful for the present. Professor Simon Rawidowicz defines it as a "revolution from within," an enterprise that defines spirituality and actualizes God's word and covenant:

> Interpretation lives by crisis in various degrees. The crisis that stimulates it will become its criterion. Interpretation can be characterized by a particular attitude of the interpreter who struggles between preserving and rejecting some forms of content of the word at his interpretative "mercy," by a tension between continuation and rebellion, tradition and innovation. It derives its strength both from a deep attachment to the "text" and from an "alienation" from it, a certain distance, a gap which has to be bridged. Interpretation is the "way out" when man is compelled to "take it" or "break it." Many a battle was fought and lost on the battlefield of interpretation. And the battle goes on and will go on as long as the person is an interpreter.[2]

The rabbinic sages as well as Jesus and his disciples shared this religious methodology by making the text a tool of expounding God's covenant and its implementation in daily existence.

Tradition and innovation inspired the vocations of innumerable generations of commentators and interpreters. They were challenged by life and history, by the very difficult task of being religious in the midst of alien traditions, confronting various kingdoms and political regimes. Persian rule gave the Jewish people political freedom to continue their covenantal existence initiated by God at Mount Sinai (Ex 20) and to explore new meanings of the relationship with God.

Religious life faced a new challenge after the triumph of Alexander the Great who conquered and dominated the whole Middle East. The king launched what amounted to an ideology of national and cultural conversion. Greek ideals in philosophy and religion, art, and culture spread to all countries conquered by Alexander, including the land of Israel. It was Athens versus Jerusalem, secular cultural values confronting the spirituality of Sinai. The battle, in many respects, goes on to the present day.

The books of the Maccabees, which were not included in the canon of the Jewish Bible, describe the Jewish struggle for the right to be different under Hellenistic domination. After Alexander, the Seleucid dynasty dominated Jerusalem; it tried to impose Hellenism on all aspects of Jewish life, including the temple, which was profaned by Greek mythological figures and idols. Hellenism also corrupted the high priesthood and Jewish leadership who fell under the spell of its customs and intellectual trends. Finally, the Jews rebelled. The rebellion was inspired by a group of spiritual leaders, the Hasidim, described in the books of Maccabees as scribes who continued Ezra's interpretative method. The Hasidim questioned and probed the will of God as laid down in the Torah tradition. One of the principles was to "make a fence around the Torah-teaching" (*Pirkei Avot* 1:1), to defend and expound God's word, creating a "tradition of the elders," which was recognized as a basic tenet of Judaism (Mk 7:3).

The Seleucid ruler Antiochus IV forbade the practice of Jewish religion. The revolt against the king was led by Mattathias, a priest who lived in Modein, near Jerusalem. It lasted two generations. When the war ended, the temple was cleansed and reconsecrated to the God of Israel. The event is recalled every year in the celebration of Hanukkah, the feast of lights, which is referred to in the gospel as well (Jn 10:22).

RELIGION AS A WAY OF BEING AND GOING

The interpreters of biblical teaching, from the time of Ezra to the second century C.E., concerned themselves with God, his commanding voice and word, and their implementation in the daily life of Israel. The interpreters' mission was to find ways and modes of making the covenantal relationship—God's election of Israel—a reality in the life of the chosen people, a continuous reality of God's love. This preoccupation resulted in a body of regulations and recommendations on how to lead a life of holiness. The methodology of sanctity they called halakah, often translated as "law" in the Greek and later on in western languages. This translation has hurt the understanding of rabbinic Judaism for two millennia.

Halakah is a noun derived from the verb *halah,* "to go." Halakah is a way of being and going, a manifestation of the covenant with God, a manner of living and reliving God's commands and partnership. Living a halakic life means to make God's presence a reality in all aspects of life: at the moment of waking up in the morning, thanking God for restoring the soul; at meals, thanking God for the goodness of food; at prayer and at study, thanking God for his presence. Halakah is the joy of being guided and shaping one's life by the experience of covenant, under the tutelage of tradition. Halakah is the discipline of being religious and living a religious existence, a way of being with God, for God.

Three religious groups dominated Jewish theological thought of the time, all of them familiar to Jesus. There may have been more, but essentially we talk of the Sadducees, the Pharisees, and the Essenes. Added to that were the Zealots, a nationalist group involved in the Jewish war of 66–73 C.E. The Sadducees originated around the third century B.C.E. and were composed largely of priests, merchants and members of the upper classes. The Sadducees controlled the clerical temple structure and many of them were members of the Sanhedrin. They followed the prescriptions of the written Torah and were opposed to any interpretation following the tradition of the oral Torah which was the rule of the Pharisees. The Sadducees emphasized the value of temple sacrifice, a reminder of the biblical offering, as a way of bringing the experience of God to the people.

The Pharisees were a unique group, a spiritual movement that renewed Jewish life after the exile (Ezra and Nehemiah) and the destruction of the second temple in 70 C.E. It became the movement of the rabbinic sages who rebuilt Judaism in the following centuries. Out of the study of the written Torah and prayer, the sages constructed an inner temple, a fortress of God that has lasted for millennia. Rabbinical thinking imparted and gives even now guidance and a vital sense of God's commands and presence to the people—in spite of such great sufferings and spiritual crises caused by Roman persecution, medieval isolation, the expulsion from Spain in 1492, and the agony of the Holocaust in our century.

The main concepts of the Pharisees are expressed symbolically in the star of David. One triangle represents God, revelation and covenant, and the other creation, peoplehood, and finally redemption. These basic ideas inspired the work of the rabbis and their attempt to make the God-Israel relationship a daily reality of the individual and the community. To believe in God is not a verbal manifestation or recognition but an exercise of the divine, inspiring each moment of the life of the Jewish person in the community and vis-à-vis other groups. Jesus reflected the Pharisaic spirit in much of his teaching.

The Essenes were a religious brotherhood up to about the second century B.C.E. By the end of the first century they were located and organized as a monastic community on the northwestern shore of the Dead Sea area. The Essenes stressed the need for personal piety and avoidance of transgression and iniquity. They believed in the immortality of the soul but rejected the concept of bodily resurrection. They were critical of the temple ritual and bureaucracy and opted for a secluded life in the wilderness of Judea as a way of implementing the covenantal relationship with God. They lived simple lives, despised luxury, and shared their property. The Essenes' monastic ways were reflected in the life of John the Baptist and influenced the followers of Jesus.

Finally, the Zealot movement was a nationalistic group. Israel was considered a theocracy by the Zealots, and their leaders asked fellow Jews not to pay tribute to Rome or acknowledge the emperor as master. Their preaching is reflected in some New Testament texts—Luke (6:15), Acts (5:37), Mark (8:33), etc.

JEWISH AND CHRISTIAN VOCATIONS: THE NEED FOR TESHUVAH

The first century marks a point of differentiation and departure in the testimony of God. There is on one side the witnessing of the Sinai covenantal relationship expressed in ritual and prayer. It is the testimony of a people chosen by God to proclaim his name in history and the human encounter. It is a *halakah* of witnessing God's covenant.

Judaism however was not indifferent to missionary work. The New Testament will later be critical of Pharisaic efforts to bring Gentiles to God, saying that they are eager to go to the other side of the world to convert one person. The missionary trend ended with Constantine's alliance with the Christian church, when Jews were forbidden any conversionary activity. The "political" triumph of Christianity ended Jewish attempts to share their experience of God with humanity. It prevented Christians from becoming familiar with Jewish spirituality and the daily reality of the God-Israel covenant. A great deal was lost to both, Judaism and Christianity, by such lack of spiritual intimacy.

The first century also was the time of another vocation to the world: Jesus bringing humanity to God. His life and commitment and his martyrdom at the hands of the Romans are signs of a calling to witness God, similar to other martyrs of faith under pagan domination. The meaning of Jesus' vocation has been interpreted by Jews through centuries. One trend of opinion was to link Noah to Jesus' mission. This was part of the medieval understanding, but mainly the work of Rabbi Elijah Benamozegh, a nineteenth century Italian rabbi and theologian.[3] Christianity, stressed Benamozegh, has a mission to the world, not to the Jews. It has to bring humanity to God and his commands and moral laws. This universal vocation, parallel to Judaism's universal witnessing of God, is linked to Noah's covenant. Benamozegh pointed out that the first covenant of God with Noah—Genesis 9—is essentially with humanity. God imposed a code of behavior. The seven Noahide laws—practice of faith and justice, avoidance of homicide, illicit intercourse, eating of living creatures, idolatry and blasphemy—are to be observed by all humanity. Noah did not fulfill his obligation and left to Jesus, according to Benamozegh, the mission to call the peoples of the world to God by following a way of holiness.

This recognition of "the other" who in faith accepts Noah's vocation is the starting point of a reflection on the Jewish perspective of Christianity's meaning and mission. It is not a definitive position.

The idea of a dual mission was already stated by the medieval sage Saadiah Ben Joseph Gaon (882–942) who said:

> The missions were twofold: one concerning Israel—"And I will take away the names of the Baalim out of her mouth." The second concerns the nations of the world, that they were destined to abandon idol worship, alluded to in the text: "And they (the Baalim) shall no more be mentioned by their name," by no single person anywhere, in accordance with the prophecy of Zephaniah (13:9): "For then will I turn to the peoples a pure language that they may all call upon the name of the Lord, to serve him with one consent."[4]

Considering Noah a precursor of Jesus' vocation does not belittle the latter's mission. Jesus' mission is conceived as part of God's call to humanity, thereby forming a bond with Jews as a community of souls testifying to God. The kingdom is not accomplished by one people alone. The very text of the book of Genesis points out the need for companionship, for a community of faith.

The contemporary Jewish theologian Joseph B. Soloveitchik describes the special sense of community by stating:

> Communities are established the very moment I recognize the thou and exchange greetings to the thou. One individual extends the "Shalom" greetings to another individual; and in so doing he creates a community . . . recognition means sacrificial action: the individual who withdraws in order to make room for the thou.[5]

This recognition of the other in faith is the starting point of a Jewish reflection on the meaning and mission of Christianity. It is not an easy task. It involves a reconsideration of the past, and a nearly prophetic hope in a joint witnessing to God. It entails on our side a return by recognition. It entails also *teshuvah,* on the Christian side a "metanoia," a change of heart that allows for the recognition of the Jewish person as part of God's design. Otherwise it is the contempt that seems to be so difficult to overcome in the religious commitment.

Teshuvah, at times translated as repentance, is a reconsideration of the past leading to a change of heart, a reinterpretation of past events in light of present insights. *Teshuvah* means a return to God, acceptance of self and fellow beings, those of our own faith as well as those with whom we share the hope of God.

Our reaction toward most of the history among Christians, quite understandably, has been pain and recrimination. In our anguish we have at times developed an inculpating triumphalism of pain, denying any possibility of encounter and friendship. *Teshuvah,* a change of heart, recognizes Christian past transgressions, but also responds affirmatively by acknowledging Christian penitence vis-à-vis Judaism. *Teshuvah* means to recall that history has changed human existence after the Second World War and that we are summoned to be together in and toward God. Emmanuel Levinas rightly pointed out the significance of such change. He said that "the existence of God is sacred history itself, the sacredness of man's relation to man through which God may pass."

To recognize the other as a person of faith is not an invitation to syncretism. It does not mean to lose one's individual commitment, but rather to strengthen particular vocations respectful of other vocations. *Teshuvah,* the change of heart, bespeaks reconsideration mindful of differences but concerned with fellowship. It is the first step, difficult by its own nature, toward encounter and communion.

AN ENCOUNTER IN FAITH

The word "encounter," frequently used in interfaith dialogue, carries some pessimistic meaning by the very origin of this word. Its root is in *contra,* against. To encounter could imply that one group stands over against another, but it can also take a more positive meaning.

An encounter between Christians and Jews can become an act of affirmation that allows two different groups to regard one another as equal partners in a process that involves learning and understanding, as well as time and space.

In the encounter of individuals there is a personal dimension of intimacy and respect. It is the background to personal encounter, common ideas or a common spirituality. This personal approach requires a recognition with the idea of establishing a community. The recognition of the other is an operation converting the "object" person to a "subject," a spiritual entity of wholeness. Rabbi Joseph B. Soloveitchik explores the idea, stating:

> Quite often a man finds himself in a crowd amongst strangers. He feels lonely. No one knows him, no one cares for him, no one is concerned with him. It is again an existential experience. He begins to doubt his ontological worth; this leads to alienation from the crowds surrounding him. Suddenly someone taps him on the shoulder and says: "Aren't you Mr. So and So? I've heard so much about you." In a fraction of a second his awareness changes. An alien being turns into a fellow member of existential community (the crowd). What brought about the change? The recognition by somebody, the word.
>
> To recognize a person is not just to identify him physically. It is more than that: it is an act of identifying him existentially, as a person who has a job to do, that only he can do properly. To recognize a person means to affirm that he is irreplaceable. To hurt a person is to tell him that he is expendable, that there is no need for him.[6]

The recognition of the other as a subject of faith, a person of God, involves a sense of responsibility, of care for the other. Rabbi Soloveitchik stresses this:

> Once I have recognized the thou and invited him to join the community, I ipso facto assume responsibility for the thou. Recognition is identical with commitment.

Here again we walk in the ways of our Maker. God created man; God did not abandon him; God showed concern for him. God cared for Adam. God said: It is not good for man to be alone. He provided him with a mate; he placed him in Paradise, and allowed him to enjoy the fruit of the Garden. Even after man sinned and was exiled from the Garden the almighty didn't desert him; of course he punished him. Yet He was concerned with man even while man was in sin. In a word, God assumed responsibility for whatever and whomever He created: "He gives bread to all flesh for His loving kindness is everlasting." (Psalm 136:25) As we have said above, the same responsibility should prevail between me and the thou whom I have recognized, and with whom I have formed a community. I assume responsibility for each member of the community to whom I have granted recognition and whom I have found worthy of being my companion. In other words the I is responsible for the physical and mental welfare of the thou.[7]

The dialogical responsibility is for a subject, a person, and not for an object. We are responsible and responsive to the other as a spiritual entity, a subject of faith, a child of God. It is a perception of mutuality for a fellow you, respectful of the integrity of the other, in which the I confirms the thou in the right of his existence and the goal of his becoming, in all his wholeness. Recognition is an invitation to be part of a community of faith, despite differences, in awareness of God's presence. Recognition is to perceive the other's meaning as a person. This is basic in human relationships, and very specially so in Jewish perception of the Christian as a person of God and partner in the search for the kingdom and its establishment in the universe. It is essentially a process of understanding and recognition of a joint human communion. Once we cease to regard the other as merely an object of observation and begin to regard him/her as an independent other, then we have the beginning of the I-Thou relationship.

Recognizing Christianity is a first step toward understanding its vocation. That is not easy for Jews because of the trauma of past experiences but indispensable on our existential road. We are not alone in the universe, no solitary islands of belief but peninsulas linked to the eternal and to one another; and there is much to learn in our respective covenantal experience of God.

Understanding leads to acceptance and mutual personal confirmation as tools of God. I have to experience the Christian person as chosen by God, with a specific task and different way, another *halakah*. I have to understand Christian fervor, "imagining the real," as Buber states: "Perceiving and thinking in the mind and body of another individual." To relate religiously to Christians means to receive "an intimation of the being of the other." It implies inclusion, embracing the other, in this case the Christian person, overcoming the over-againstness of previous history. To relate religiously is to fathom the mystery of the present Christian-Jewish interchange, called dialogue, until a new word will be developed to describe the very meaning of the present encounter.[8]

Maurice Friedman in his introduction to Martin Buber's *Daniel* focuses on the projection of the Jewish perception of Christianity. To experience the other

> means to feel an event from the side of the person one meets as well as from one's own side. It is an inclusiveness which realizes the other person in the actuality of his being, but it must not be identified with "empathy," which means transposing oneself into the dynamic structure of an object, hence, as Buber says, "the exclusion of one's own concreteness, the extinguishing of the actual situation of life, its absorption in pure aestheticism of the reality in which one participates." Inclusion is the opposite of this. "It is the extension of one's own concreteness, the fulfillment of the actual situation of life, the complete presence of the reality in which one participates." In [the process of] inclusion, one person, "without fulfilling any thing of the felt reality of this activity, at the same time lives through the common event from the standpoint of the other."[9]

Encounter as relationship is the acceptance of the other as a being in faith, a person with his own rights and his own commitments. We deal with persons, not objects. It is the communion of the spirit, not a relationship as with an object. Encounter is a process of the heart, from disdain to recognition, from alienation to creative proximity. It entails an evolution from confrontation toward a challenging relationship of equals, the starting point of spiritual healing.

Martin Buber in his book *Two Types of Faith* rightly pointed out the importance of the Christian and Jewish vocations in encounter:

> The faith of Judaism and the faith of Christendom are by nature different in kind, each in conformity with its human basis, and they will indeed remain different, until mankind is gathered from the exiles of the religions into a kinship of God. But Israel striving after the renewal of its faith through the rebirth of the person and Christianity striving for the renewal of its faith through the rebirth of nations will have some-

thing as yet unsaid to say to each other and help to give to one another —hardly to be conceived at the present time.[10]

The present collection of essays on Christianity by Jewish theologians attempts exactly that: to talk to one another, the beginning of a unique communion of faith with respect for differences.

NOTES

1. Helga Croner, ed., *Stepping Stones to Further Jewish-Christian Relations* (London-New York: Stimulus Foundation, 1977), pp. 173–174.

2. Simon Rawidowitz, *Studies in Jewish Thought* (Philadelphia: The Jewish Publication Society 1974), p. 45.

3. E. Benamozegh, *Morale Juive et Morale Chrétienne* (Firenze: Casa Editrice Israel, 1925); *Israel et l'Humanité* (Paris: Payot, 1914).

4. Nehama Leibowitz, *Studies in Bamidbar* (Jerusalem: The World Zionist Organization, 1980), p. 37.

5. Joseph B. Soloveitchik, "The Community," *Tradition* (New York: Spring 1978), p. 15.

6. Ibid. p. 16.

7. Ibid. pp. 18–19.

8. Donald L. Berry, *Mutuality: The Vision of Martin Buber* (Albany: State University of New York Press, 1985), p. 43.

9. Martin Buber, *Daniel* (New York: McGraw-Hill Paperbacks, 1965), p. 33.

10. Martin Buber, *Two Types of Faith* (New York: Harper Torch Books, 1951), pp. 173–174.

Themes in Christian-Jewish Relations

Norman Solomon

INTRODUCTION: THE LANGUAGES WE SPEAK

There is no abstract entity "Judaism" or "Christianity" but rather two complex, overlapping cultural systems with bundles of words at their foci. There is a Jewish language, and a Christian language, and dialects of each, and each interacts with the "natural languages"[1] of people, and they vary in the following ways:

1. Each language has key terms. An orthodox religious Jew might use a set consisting of: God, *torah, mitzva,* free will, *teshuva, tefilla, tsedaka, hesed, yetser tov (ra)*, Israel.[2] A liberal religious Jew or a secular Jew would have a different set, and the many varieties of Christian would have their individual, overlapping sets.

2. Even where the same term is used in more than one language, it may have a different range of meaning attached to it. Thus "salvation" is used by both Jews and Christians; sometimes they use it in the same way, sometimes not.

3. Even where a term has much the same range of meaning in one language as in another, the weight attached to the term may be very different in one from the other. "Messiah" (in Greek, *Christos*), for instance, is a very weighty term for Christians—indeed, it may not be possible to have a Christian language without it. Among Jews the term carries less weight; it is important rather than central (an arm or leg, rather than the heart, of the body of Judaism).

4. The specific language of the religious culture is a restricted one; it is a sub-set of the natural language, such as English, of the speaker (clearly, English contains far more than the varieties of Christian language which it

16

incorporates). It may not, for instance, be possible to talk within the language of Christianity about distinctively Jewish concepts such as those of Torah and *mitzva,* or to talk within the language of Judaism about Christ or incarnation. But one can talk about them in English, for English may be indefinitely extended so as to include them.

5. An individual speaker may talk tolerably well about more than one religion, for his total language may include the languages of more than one religion, even though he personally attaches himself to just one. To talk better than tolerably is extremely difficult, for weights as well as meanings of words have to be handled, and the meanings themselves are affected by the context of the language as a whole. The overall language may simply be a natural language which has assimilated vocabularies of both religions, including the multiple range of meaning of individual terms. Or it may be a specialized sub-language such as the English of philosophy, anthropology, history or sociology.

Clearly, when we examine the relationship between Judaism and Christianity, it will be necessary to climb beyond the limitations of any of our individual religious languages.[3]

This said, I will now discuss this relationship under five themes that repeatedly surface in conversations with one another: covenant, redemption, Holocaust, state of Israel, and Jewish-Christian dialogue today.

I. COVENANT

When one says that Christianity and Judaism claim to be covenantal faiths, is one saying the same thing about each? Does each make the same claim? This can only be answered by exploring "from within" the generally received texts of each religion and then talking about them in a language broad enough to contain both sets of texts but not itself dominated by either. So it is not germane to our purpose to explore, with Bible scholars, the linkage between Bronze Age Hittite suzerainty treaties and the biblical concept of *brit,* nor even to establish an historically correct reading of the Hebrew scriptures. What matters is how "covenant" is understood by the rabbis, the church fathers, and their respective successors, and that we avoid imposing on the discussion a framework which is determined by either tradition.

1. The Grammar of "Covenant"

A covenant is an agreement—a binding agreement.

It is therefore entered into by two parties, individuals or groups. The parties to the covenant are not necessarily equal. In biblical usage, in particular, God is the superior party; hence covenant involves grace on his part.

One party needs the covenant, the other does not.

Still, there are obligations and gifts on both sides—a covenant is reciprocal, if not equal. Mankind (Abraham, for instance) will obey God; in return, God will protect the human partner(s).

Whole chunks of biblical legislation are apparently "conditions," "small print," of covenants. For instance, the legislation in Deuteronomy 12–28 constitutes the "terms" of the covenant of Deuteronomy 29. However, the question remains open of the primacy of covenant or law. Christian theologians always write as if the covenant were the prime concern, and the law "small print." Traditional Jews read with a very different emphasis. The law stands in its own right, God's gracious gift for our benefit. That God has favored us with a covenant is an additional blessing, a sign of his love; but what really matters is his guidance as expressed in the law.

2. The Hebrew Scriptures

A plain reading of the Hebrew scriptures makes it look as if there are numerous covenants, as if God were trying desperately to make a lasting covenant with somebody—with Noah, several times with Abraham, with Israel, with David, with Aaron, with Joshua, Josiah and Ezra—and having great trouble in making any one covenant stick. This is what Jeremiah worries about when he promises a new and lasting covenant: "I will set my law within them and write it on their hearts" (31:33).

But a covenant relationship is inherently unstable. God owes a covenant to no one, and no human partner can be relied upon to fulfill the terms of the covenant constantly. Much of the Bible revolves around the dynamic generated by this instability. The dynamic has been well brought out by Dan Jacobson in *The Story of the Stories*:[4] from the perspective of a writer rather than a theologian or Bible scholar he sees the "story" as working out the tension between the desire to be chosen and the fear of being chosen.

Jacob B. Agus[5] points out that the "prophets were uncomfortable with the notion of setting conditions for and limitations upon God's will. God's relations with Israel were due to God's goodness, love and compassion."

It really is important to understand that "covenant," in both Hebrew

Bible and Jewish theology, is just one possible model of the relationship between God and humankind (individual, national, or universal). As Agus says, the biblical authors were well aware of the limitations of the model, and hence often qualify it with such terms as *hesed* (love) and *shalom* (peace).[6]

3. The Christians

I hear Christians talking about *"the* covenant," as if there was just one covenant—or, at least, just one of special significance. If a Christian assumes there is just one covenant of major significance, he worries whether *the* covenant continued with Christians in place of the "old" Israel, or whether *the* covenant with Israel was broadened—or whether after all there are *two* covenants, one of them perhaps the covenant with Abel.

"Covenant" has become an idol, a metaphysical something that seems to exist apart from people. Indeed, one of the greatest difficulties Jews find in conversing with Christians about theology is the way that Christians attach extraordinary weight and emotional significance to terms which, among Jews, seem to be normal everyday words whose precise definition is a not a matter of great importance. It feels as though the person one is talking to has an obsession with the term. It is not that Christians are more obsessive than any other people, but rather that typically the objects of their special worry turn out to be words which can be given theological connotations. So far as the word "covenant" is concerned, the process was initiated by Paul, who, in "contrasting the covenant of Abraham with that of Moses and the covenant of the spirit with that of the letter, set the stage for a bitter polemic with the Jewish Sages."[7] Presumably in reply to this the sages emphasize that our father Abraham kept all the commandments of the Torah,[8] i.e. the covenant of Moses— there was no contrast between the covenants, which were complementary. Of course, this notion in turn was adapted to the Christian way of thinking—that Abraham, and for that matter Christians, kept all the commandments "according to the spirit"—or it may be that it was the Jews in this case who were turning a Christian notion to their own purposes.

4. The Rabbis

When Jews are not reacting to Christians they tend not to talk in this way about *the* covenant, but in the plain biblical way about numerous covenants. They are conspicuously unworried about the term. Certainly, major Jewish philosophers of religion such as Maimonides have virtually nothing to say about it.[9]

The plain truth seems to be that "covenant" is not a key term in Judaism. Only the imposition of a Christian agenda generates serious discussion about it.

The rabbis talk of thirteen covenants in connection with circumcision alone.[10] Covenants are made, broken, renewed. The lack of a covenant which is irrevocable per se creates anxiety, as was explained in section 2. If the covenant is not permanent, what is? The rabbis do not formulate this question, but the answer is implied in their stress on God's love for Israel, and the merits of the fathers—these are the guarantee that God will keep his promises notwithstanding our imperfections.

From the story of Achan (Jos 7) we learn that "a Jew, though he sin, is still a Jew." This is perhaps an oblique reference to Christian claims that Israel's sins had lost her the covenant, and thus an early instance of the pressure of Christian agenda.

(a) Space for Christianity

Recent writers have attempted to subsume Christianity and Islam under a "Noahide covenant." The germ of this attitude goes back to Halevi and Maimonides; Halevi (c. 1075–1141), for instance, recognizes a role in God's plan for the other monotheistic religions, for "they serve to introduce and pave the way for the expected Messiah, who is the fruition, and they will all become his fruit."[11,12]

The idea of the Noahide covenant itself is even older, for the Talmud, without reference to Christianity or Islam, lists "seven commandments (*mitzvot*) of the children of Noah (i.e. all humanity, who are descended from him)"—viz., not to worship idols, not to blaspheme, not to commit murder, adultery or theft, not to treat animals with cruelty, and to set up courts of law.[13]

The contemporary orthodox rabbi David Hartman has proposed an interesting development of this approach.[14] He finds in the Bible two covenants, that of creation and that of Sinai. The creation covenant (reflected in that of Noah) is with all mankind, universal and for all time. The Sinai covenant is with Israel, and does not preclude other, parallel covenants with other societies. This allows for a plurality of revelations, each of them God's way of addressing himself to a particular group of people.

It is, of course, for the modern theologian to extend the traditional religious language to cover new situations and insights. This is what Hartman and the others are doing, and it is certainly legitimate.

However, traditional rabbinic talk about *bnei Noah* (children of Noah = all humankind) uses *mitzva* language, not covenant language. In fact, the specific Noahide commandments are derived from verses in Genesis 2 as well as from the opening verses of Genesis 9 which actually *precede* mention of the rainbow covenant. The way the rabbis read the passage, it is the commandments which are to the fore; the covenant depends on the commandments rather than vice versa.

From the rabbinic point of view, the question as to whether Christians might be subsumed under some covenant is rather fatuous. What do they need a covenant for? Indeed, in envying us our covenant they are envying the wrong thing. If anything, they might envy our *mitzvot*. Then let them start with the seven they have, and if any individual desires the full 613 he is welcome to join Israel. One of the tragedies of Christian covenant envy is that it has so often led to appropriation, to a theological robbery of "*the* covenant." If only Christians envied our *mitzvot* instead, they would not need to steal anything or displace anybody in God's favor; we could by all means all observe God's commands together.

(b) Belief and Salvation

That notoriously unreliable second century C.E. biographer Diogenes Laertius attributes to both Thales and Socrates the following saying: "I thank Tyche that I was born a human being and not an animal, a man and not a woman, a Greek and not a barbarian."[15] Paul had already said: "There is no such thing as Jew and Greek, slave and freeman, male and female; for you are all one person in Christ Jesus" (Gal 3:28). The context of faith versus law in which this remark is set has led to its being popularly understood, notwithstanding learned demurral, to mean that belief in Christ Jesus was that which saved—belief, not deeds. Belief is the criterion of God's favor, and it is the line of demarcation between the issue of Abraham and other people. Probably the same popular saying which underlay both Socrates and Paul was behind the rabbinic version, which runs: "I call to witness heaven and earth that whether 'goy' or Jew, whether man or woman, whether manservant or maidservant, it is entirely according to the deeds of the individual that the heavenly spirit rests upon him."[16] The rabbis are, in effect, taking Ezekiel's stress on individual responsibility (particularly chapter 18) and giving it universal application; almost certainly they were commenting (if indirectly) on Paul, and rejecting his stress on correct belief.

But if we set aside the Pauline emphasis on the exclusiveness of salvation through faith in Christ—in other words, if we set aside the Christian agenda—there is no particular problem left in finding "theological space" for people who do not have that faith.

5. A Christian Covenant Acknowledged?

The question is sometimes asked whether a Christian covenant could be acknowledged in Jewish terms—and if so, how. This is an instance of the imposition of a Christian agenda and understanding on Judaism. Within Judaism, there is no need to provide a special covenant to ensure God's grace, but covenants (rainbow, creation) are available for theologians to apply to mankind in general should they so wish. The real point from the Jewish perspective is a different one—what are the *mitzvot* applicable to all humanity? It is primarily through these that God has expressed his care for human society and the environment.

As a Jew, I do not have to legitimate some special covenant in order to appreciate fully the devotion of Christians to God or to assess whether their way of life might be pleasing in God's eyes.

II. REDEMPTION

In the following I shall make no sustained attempt to sort out the distinctions between terms such as "save" and "redeem," or among the range of corresponding Hebrew verbs such as *pada, hitsil, ga'al,* and *hoshi'a.* What matters is the broad concept.

1. The Grammar of "Save"

Both "save" and "redeem" can cover:

(a) To get people out of captivity, free of foreign domination or occupation, to restore them to their land, to make them free.

(b) To get an individual out of a stressful situation—either physical or mental distress, threat, sickness, or sin (guilt), alienation from God.

This much is clear in the Hebrew scriptures, and nowhere more beautifully and powerfully expressed than in the psalms.

Some Christians maintain that "The lack of love, both given and received, keeps human beings in need of salvation."[17] This seems to me a way of drawing attention to a common aspect of several (but not all) of the situations listed above. However, it is confusing as concerns other types. For instance, if I fall over and break a bone in my arm I am not necessarily suffering from a lack of love—perhaps everybody loves me, even God (who no doubt means it for my own good). I don't need more love to "redeem" me from that; I need a skillful surgeon.

Another problem with reducing everything to the absence or presence of love is that it fails to draw attention to the specifics of the situation, and hence cannot be specific about the cure. Sin surely implies a failing in love of God on the part of the sinner; but to get out of it an increase of love is not much use unless directed by the specifics of penitence.

2. The Christian Cosmic Jump

The concept of redemption, then, relates to the particular type of situation from which it is envisaged that the individual should be saved. What are listed above are either national catastrophes or personal problems. Since Paul, however, Christians have conceived of an even greater distress. Paul—for instance Romans 7:7–25—sees man not just as liable to sin, but as the slave of sin. Sin is in his view not merely *yetser hara,* an evil tendency, but a master. At a later stage of Christian development, notably in Revelation, sin, the master, takes clear shape, becomes a power, an externalized force of evil. Combining this with an identification of the serpent in Genesis as the devil, and with a false genetics according to which all future people were quite literally within the seed of Adam, it was easy for Augustine[18] to develop a doctrine of "original sin" according to which Adam's fall was a cosmic one in which we all participated and from which only a once-for-all act of cosmic redemption could save us. True, Justin and Tatian both saw Adam's sin as a prototype rather than an actual inherited taint, and Clement of Alexandria vigorously denies that a newborn baby which has not performed any act of its own can have fallen under the curse of Adam.[19] Modern Christians may build new theologies on the non-Augustinian sources, but the "cosmic mess-up" theory dies hard, and still numbers many followers.

3. Cosmic Redemption in Jewish Mysticism

So strong was the influence of Christian cosmic evil/cosmic redemption theory that it was absorbed (without conscious recognition of its source) by the Jewish mystics.

Rabbi Isaac Luria,[20] for instance, saw the exile not only "as a terrible and pitiless state permeating and embittering all of Jewish life, but . . . (as) the condition of the universe as a whole, even of the deity."[21] Not only Israel, but the cosmos, and, indeed, the creator, were in exile—a concept which can be traced back easily to rabbinic statements[22] attributed to sages of the second century. But although the rabbis recognized the "divine pathos"[23]—God's fellow-feeling, so to speak, with Israel—they did not take Luria's further step of universalizing the concept of exile; for them *galut* (exile) was essentially the experience of Israel at the hand of the nations, not an experience shared by the nations.

That Luria took this step is a consequence of his extraordinary theory of creation. According to this theory, God creates by simultaneously (a) limiting himself, so as to "make room" for something other than himself, and (b) emanating light into the empty space so formed.[24] But the vessels into which God, in the process of creation, emanated the pristine light were not strong enough to contain it. As they shattered, some of the light returned to its origin, but the rest, consisting of "sparks," was scattered in confusion, putting *galut* (exile = alienation, displacement) into the very heart of created things. Some of the light even fell into "husks," "shells," which inhabit the abyss of evil, the "empty space" from which God withdrew himself; these sparks aspire to rise from the darkness and return to their source, but cannot do so without help. Thus God himself, so to speak, has partly "fallen" into exile.

4. The Mitzvot

In classical Jewish sources *mitzvot* are not presented as "redemption," though they certainly are, as we shall see shortly, in later Jewish mysticism. In mainstream Judaism, however, the *mitzvot* are a means to *zechut,* uncomfortably translated "merit"—that is, to ensuring a proper and wholesome relationship with God by conforming to his will as expressed in revelation.

Modern Jewish theologians might refer to this process as "fulfillment" rather than "salvation." Such a distinction is not without problems. It would be very difficult to find any rabbinic word corresponding to "fulfillment"; one suspects that in the attempt to avoid Christian vocabulary in describing Judaism these theologians have taken hold of modern psychological jargon in its place. The redemption/fulfillment contrast of which they speak is a symptom not so much of the difference between Judaism and Christianity as of that between classical Jewish and Christian ways of talk on the one hand and modern psychological discourse on the other.

True, one can read Maimonides' *Guide* and conclude that the *mitz-*

vot are the tools to enable one to approach individual perfection ever more closely in the contemplative life.

But then there is a considerable body of rabbinic sayings throughout the ages presenting the *mitzvot* as "antidote" to sin, or to the *yetser hara,* for instance the talmudic: "The Holy One, blessed be He, said to Israel, 'I created the *yetser hara,* and I created the Torah as a medicine against it.' "[25]

We have referred previously to Isaac Luria's philosophy of the cosmic flaw built in to the world at its creation. What is the way of redemption from this, the way "out of the mess"?

Luria's exotic and extravagant kabbalism springs to life as soon as we place it in the context of the experiences and hopes of sixteenth century Jewry. Life, with all its suffering and disappointment, was given new meaning; it became comprehensible and therefore acceptable. Our exile was the embodiment of the "fallen sparks" of creation captured within the "husks" of impurity; the divine light of these sparks within us was striving to return godward. With the assurance that every time a Jew performed a *mitzva* he restored some of this light to its place of origin it became possible for him to see that the redemption had already begun, that it was a continuous process in which every Jew, however humble, was privileged to participate. Thus the everyday minutiae of Jewish life, the study of the torah, the observance of the dietary laws and all the ceremonies—matters perhaps irksome to the downtrodden Jew and ridiculed by his Christian or Muslim overlords—became the actual vehicle of cosmic redemption. To tie on one's *tefillin* correctly, to pray with full devotion and in carefully formulated words—these were no longer merely (as if it would not have been enough) a means to satisfactory individual expression of the love of God; they were momentous acts of universal significance, for the whole world, whether it cared to know it or not, stood or fell by Israel's performance of the commandments.

The process of restoration of light is *tiqqun* (mending, restoration). Whoever performs a *mitzva* mends not only himself and Israel but all of God's creation.

5. Faith or Fulfillment?

A word takes meaning from its context, and we saw that "salvation," in Christian talk, is colored by "original sin."

The traditional Christian question about whether people are "saved" by faith makes little sense in Jewish terms. Characteristically, the rabbis, like the second century Joshua and Gamaliel II,[26] when they want to discuss the status of non-Israelites in the eyes of God, ask not whether they are "saved" but whether they "have a share in the world to come." Unfortunately Jewish apologists tend to pick up the way of talk of the Christians to whom they address themselves, and one frequently reads in their works words to the effect that "In Judaism, all that a non-Jew is expected to do *in order to be saved* is to observe the seven Noahide commandments." This is careless, and an inaccurate representation of the words of the rabbis, who we can now see were deliberate, perhaps even polemical, in talking of a "portion in the world to come" rather than of "being saved."

It is true that the rabbis stressed way of conduct rather than belief in theological propositions. Still, they listed heretics and unbelievers as having "no share in the world to come,"[27] they stressed the value of *emunah* (trust in God), and they constantly emphasized our dependence on God's *hesed* (love, grace) in assisting our weak efforts to serve him.

Christians, even at the height of the reformation controversies on faith and works, rarely went so far as to deny all significance to works— and the Catholic Church in any case rejected the claims of reformers such as Luther and Calvin on this point.

One must conclude that redemption through faith or fulfillment through *mitzvot* is a simplistic generalization of the distinction between Christian and Jewish attitudes. The considerable overlap between the two faiths is obscured by their different terminologies and emphases.

III. HOLOCAUST

1. Christian Moral Credibility

It is frequently alleged that the modern scientific worldview was finally refuted at Auschwitz.[28] After all, the Germans were a leading nation in science, technology and culture, and this did not stop them from committing atrocities; indeed, it enabled them to carry out their atrocities with greater technical and administrative efficiency.

This argument is equivalent to blaming the invention of the telephone for the telling of lies or for the spread of gossip and slander. The telephone does not speak. People speak. The telephone is neutral. It is the people who use it who are responsible for lies or truth, for defamation or praise.

Likewise, it is not science and technology which are refuted by Auschwitz, but the morality of the perpetrators. Of course, if it could be shown that the Nazi morality was derived from and a reasonable consequence of the new insights and discoveries of the scientific and cultural revolution, one would have to approach that revolution with great circumspection. But there is no connection between the two. True, the Nazis utilized certain biological theories about race to justify their aims. However, not only were these theories actually wrong but, even if true, would not necessarily provide any foundation for Nazism; it does not follow that because one race is superior to another it has to destroy it—other assumptions have to be introduced to justify such a conclusion.

A "refutation" of enlightenment ideas on the inevitability of progress is likewise not a refutation of the scientific and cultural revolution. In fact, it is part of that revolution. The cynicism and despair of which we have seen much this century may have been accentuated by the Holocaust and other human tragedies, but the negative side of the human character had already been demonstrated by depth psychologists well before Hitler came to power.

But all this concerns ideologists. What were the sources of the moral standards of ordinary Germans of the Shoah period? So far as ordinary Germans were concerned, the church was a far stronger source for morality than the bourgeois *Kultur* of which, paradoxically, Jews were often leading standard-bearers. Undoubtedly the churches were a major contributor to popular ideas of right and wrong; after all, over ninety percent of Germans attended church regularly. They read the Bible, they heard the sermons.

The voice that called for the "final solution" was the voice of the pagan, Hitler. But the hands that implemented it were the hands of ordinary Christians. In fact, it is very hard to document from Nazi sources any definition of the "final solution" as being the total humiliation and destruction of the Jews. The conclusion has to be that Christians did not need this spelled out for them; they knew what to do, but it would have been embarrassing to make it explicit.

Of course, many conscientious Christians resisted. But they were individuals, not churches.

So, it is not the modern scientific world view which lost moral credibility at Auschwitz, but traditional Christianity and its churches.

That traditional Christianity is not "true" Christianity is not for Jews to decide but for contemporary Christians to demonstrate.

(a) The Link—The Teaching of Contempt

Neither the reticence of the churches in opposing the destruction of the Jews nor the readiness of ordinary Christians to implement the *Shoah* was accidental.

Hitler's core message about the Jews was Christian; only his methods were not. (There were of course other differences, but from the victim's point of view they were not very important. For instance, the inquisitor had tortured and killed out of Christian love, for the benefit of his victim's immortal soul; Hitler did not preach a religion of love.)

In his early writings and speeches Hitler, seeking the support of the masses, spoke overtly Christian language. "Hence I believe that I am acting in accordance with the will of the Almighty Creator: *by defending myself against the Jew, I am fighting for the word of the Lord.*"[34] His attacks on Jews and Judaism were consciously expressed in the language of traditional Christian antisemitism and the infamous laws of Nuremberg consciously modeled on the legislation of the medieval church. It *was* the church that had instigated trade restrictions against the Jew (a direct model for the Nazi boycott of April 1, 1933), and the ghetto and the yellow badge; it *was* Christians who first utilized the blood libel as an excuse to murder Jews.[30] It was the church that sewed into the fabric of western culture the images and stereotypes of the Jew that allowed so many of its faithful sons to accept without demur the alienation and vilification of the Jew preached by Hitler. For it was the church whose gospel concerning the Jews was, as Jules Isaac called it, *l'enseignement du mépris,* the teaching of contempt. Hitler's *Judenhaß* was not significantly greater than that of Luther—and it has taken all the courage of the post-holocaust Lutheran Church to repudiate that aspect of the "great reformer's" teaching.[31]

(b) Appropriation

In reality there is an inherent ambiguity in the Christian situation in the Holocaust. It is beyond any shadow of doubt that the ultimate aim of the Nazis was totally to destroy Christianity—though not Christian people who, unlike Jews, could be Aryans and thus "save" themselves by abjuring Christianity.

The Roman Catholic Church at the present time seems intent on creating an image of itself as victim of the Holocaust, if not to the same extent as the Jews. The beatifications of Maximilian Kolbe and Edith Stein belong to the church's search for its own Holocaust martyrs. In Poland the process is a natural enough one. Auschwitz has become, to Poles, a national symbol of suffering under the Nazis, and Polish Catholics now come there to pray and to seek atonement and reconciliation.

After all, Auschwitz was set up as a concentration camp for (non-Jewish) Poles, and hundreds of thousands of them perished there.

One asks, therefore, why Jews reacted so strongly to the siting of a Carmelite convent in the "Old Theatre" on the perimeter of the Auschwitz site. Why did they see the Catholic presence at Auschwitz as the appropriation of a uniquely Jewish symbol—worse, as the oppressor donning the garb of the victim? Why do Jews find it so hard to recognize Christians in general (they are very ready to note the exceptions) as their brothers and sisters in suffering?

The fact is that Jews tend to view the Shoah as the culmination of their degradation and persecution at the hand of Christians. They see Christians by and large as persecutors, with a relatively small number as victims and an even smaller number showing the least concern for Jewish victims. Since the Holocaust, Jews have ceased to take the moral credibility of the church seriously.

Yet a recent consultation of Jews and Catholics in Poland was remarkable for the way in which both Jews and Catholics began to share the sense of brotherhood in suffering, even though—perhaps because—it was recognized that the church had made errors of both omission and commission. To stand at Auschwitz, as I did, with the archbishop of Cracow and the assembled company of Jews and Catholics, and to recite *kaddish* together, was an act of joint sorrow and reconciliation, not a sweeping aside of the past nor a false appropriation. It was a sign that a new understanding and constructive relationship is possible.

2. The Jewish Response

On the basis of the foregoing it is evident that Jews see the Holocaust as the culmination of the centuries of Christian "teaching of contempt"; the response is the culmination of Jewish rejection of Christian moral credibility. That is, no Christian, simply in virtue of being a Christian believer, is accorded moral credibility, let alone superiority. The individual Christian rather may earn such credibility through the conduct of his own personal life. Those who helped Jews during the Holocaust are given special honor, as in the Memorial to the Righteous Gentiles at *Yad Vashem;* they are seen to have triumphed as individuals, not as Christians.

Such a view is harsh toward Christians. While it contains too much truth to be ignored, the way forward lies in recognizing that Christianity is a complex cultural construct, diverse in its manifestations, and though

Christendom has indeed nurtured the "teaching of contempt" in its bosom, there have been and certainly are today many other Christian approaches to Jews. Even though the New Testament and the fathers lend themselves readily to an anti-Jewish interpretation—sometimes, particularly with the fathers, inescapably so—resources are available from within Christianity to develop a constructive relationship with Jews and Judaism.

Jews have responded positively to post-holocaust opportunities for dialogue with Christians, and often taken the initiative themselves.

To a considerable extent the contemporary dialogue is a vehicle for the joint assertion of ethical and spiritual values in today's society,[32] and involves at the least a mutual recognition of each other's integrity and an acceptance of the idea that God (or the "Holy Spirit") continues to speak through people of different faiths. The dialogue, after all, commenced before the Shoah.

However, as Fackenheim has eloquently put it: "Christianity is ruptured by the Holocaust and stands in need of a *Tikkun*. . . . Surely the Christian good news that God saves in Christ is itself broken by *this* news."[33] The repentance required of Christians in order that authentic dialogue may take place is not, Fackenheim avers, merely a repentance of the open antisemitism which led to Auschwitz, but something far more radical. It is a "repentance of supersessionism vis-à-vis Judaism and the Jewish people."[34] As the Christian A. Roy Eckardt puts it: "Decisively, Christians view the witness of the New Testament as pointing to the historical-divine consummation of the expectations of the so-called Old Testament (Hebrew scripture, the *Tanak*) and hence as a fulfillment of, and judgment upon, Judaism and Jewishness."[35] It is this element of "judgment" which fed the antisemitism of Christendom over the ages, and which, notwithstanding its manifest irrelevance to Jews beyond the New Testament narrative, persists in many Christian theologies today. Eckardt discusses five christological models offered by theologians whom he praises for their vigorous opposition to the "teaching of contempt," and finds them all wanting; for, in his view, they fail to overcome the supersessionism which is the generating force of antisemitism.[36] Paradoxically, it may be that a new and adequate christology can only be created, if at all, together with Jews.

Yet, on the other hand, Jews must beware of imposing a particular christology on Christians with whom they engage in dialogue. It is ultimately up to Christians to define themselves, and to decide to what extent some form of "supersessionism" is unavoidable. Cardinal Willebrands, clarifying an article by Cardinal Ratzinger[37] which had caused much offense to Jews, stated: "We acknowledge and respect the Jewish people in its own faith and expectation" and "Through dialogue we hope to overcome misunderstandings, the teaching of contempt in order to develop true knowledge, respect and love." It would be wrong for Jews to ask more than this. Indeed, so long as we Jews believe in the ultimate theological superiority of our own faith and expect Christians to engage in dialogue with us on the basis that we so believe, we cannot expect them to abandon their own beliefs in the interest of the dialogue. Of course, there are many Jews and Christians who in any case take a "relativist" position, denying that any theology is ultimately superior to any other; but for such people dialogue is in any case not problematic.

IV. ISRAEL AND ESCHATOLOGY

1. The New Confidence

For Jews the rise of the state of Israel has brought a new confidence, in stark opposition to the despair of the Shoah. Yet the determination with which this confidence has sometimes been expressed indicates that fears and insecurity remain, as indeed they are likely to so long as Israel is threatened by its neighbors with destruction, and many nations of the world—not to speak of church bodies—are hesitant in its support.

The growth of Jewish self-confidence has affected dialogue with Christians in two ways. On the one hand, Jews have felt less threatened by dialogue and been more ready to take part in it. On the other hand, some Jews have abandoned what they consider an apologetic stance and see no point in dialogue.

2. The Refutation of Triumphalism

The establishment of the Jewish state is not the only instance of Jewish empowerment in the modern world. Jews, as individuals, have had prominent and powerful roles to play in most western democracies and even in eastern Europe. However, the state of Israel is the only example of *collective* Jewish empowerment.

Precisely this form of empowerment has been most strongly and consistently denied in the Christian tradition. Justin Martyr, for instance, declares: "The Jews have therefore been dispossessed of the promised land forever, and henceforth they must be perpetual exiles."[38] Or Jerome:

"You *have* what you chose. Until the end of the world you shall serve Caesar. Until the full number of the Gentiles shall come in and so all Israel shall be saved."[39] Even more influential and authoritative are the words of Augustine, commenting on Genesis: "Here no one can fail to see that in every land where the Jews are scattered, they mourn for the loss of their kingdom and are in terrified subjection to the immensely superior number of Christians. . . . To the end of the seven days of time the continued preservation of the Jews will be a proof to believing Christians of the subjection merited by those who, in the pride of their kingdom, put the Lord to death."[40]

Therefore, the establishment of the Jewish state is the strongest form of refutation of traditional Christian triumphalism.

But it may be doubted that the refutation of triumphalism is the soundest foundation on which to base a relationship with Christians. Evidently it makes them feel uncomfortable. Hence the convolutions and hesitancies on the part of mainstream Christian bodies in relating themselves to the state of Israel, their inability to achieve normality in such a relationship and to "detheologize" it effectively.

3. Call to Christians To Stop Theologizing Jews

The very existence of the state of Israel challenges Christians to overcome their anti-Jewish bias and respond normally to the state. But this is precisely what many of them find difficult to do. Double standards of judgment are readily applied to Israel, for expectations are colored by biblical interpretations. It is not surprising that Israel often falls short of such expectations. But can Christians *normalize* their reactions, or do they inevitably slip into the double trap?

One side of the trap snares the "literalists," those who see the return to Zion as fulfillment of prophecy, and whose uncritical enthusiasm for the state embarrasses its reasonable supporters. They also believe that Jews will be converted, though they differ as to whether Christians should directly encourage the process of conversion or merely wait on the sidelines.[41]

The other side is occupied by those of more subtle prejudice, those who subconsciously still look for opportunities to discredit Jews. The extreme manifestation of this syndrome is the anti-Zionist who stresses that he (or she, for Christian feminism has often fallen at this point) is not against Jews as such, but whose anti-Zionism is a sublimated antisemitism. For there is much guilt among Christians with regard to Jews, not only following the Holocaust, but arising from the primal Christian self-awareness as displacing Jews in God's plan. It is this guilt which is easily off-loaded onto Jews under stress.

What both of these groups have conspicuously failed to do is to de-theologize Israel, to look at it as a normal human being might look at any other nation. They have not freed themselves from their "hang-up" about Jews, a hang-up which arises from seeing Jews as theological objects rather than as real people.

4. Jewish Views of the Land

Several ways of looking at the return to the land of Israel are current among Jews, and not all have an eschatological dimension. In particular, the two extremes are non-eschatological. The secular extreme rejects religious eschatology in principle, and looks on Israel as any other national state; its nearest approach to eschatology is socialist utopianism. The religious extreme, as represented by the Rabbi of Sotmar, does hold eschatological views, and is imbued with longing for the ultimate messianic redemption; but it sees the present, "secular" state of Israel as an irrelevance, even as a distraction from the true "things of the end time."

Far more common among traditional Jews is the sort of view espoused and developed by Rabbi Abraham Isaac Kook (1865–1935), the first chief rabbi of Palestine in modern times. The present state of Israel[42] may be imperfect (though not more so than other nation states), but it is a "commencement of redemption," a God-given move in history to bring about universal peace for all humankind and, moreover, a move in which we are privileged to take part by working individually to ensure that society in the state is guided by the values and teachings of Torah.

This view, which derives from the Lurianic stream of kabbala to which reference was made is parallel with Christianity in one remarkable feature. For, to Christians, the work of Christ is not yet complete, only begun; the *eschaton* remains unrealized. Whether a second coming is envisaged, or some other way of completion, the fulfillment of God's kingdom on earth still awaits his gracious and loving intervention.

Several dangers beset any "commencement of redemption" view. One of the main ones is that, when redemption is not completed, the *eschaton* not realized, people stop waiting for God and take matters into their own hands. Hence Augustine, in the newly arrived Constantinian *tempora Christiana,* did not attend upon the Holy Spirit to inspire the Donatists, but enlisted the help of Count Boniface to crush Christian dissidence by force, for *quae peior mors animae quam libertas erroris.*[43] Likewise, Rav Kook's followers lack the patience of the master, and translate his vision of Israel as a beacon of peace and holiness among the nations into the *Gush Emunim* philosophy of the duty, seeing the power is available, to take the initiative in settling the land (though not, be it noted, to initiate conquest).

There is also the danger of reading the Bible as a series of proof-texts for contemporary events, and of then "jumping on God's bandwagon" and attempting to force events into the predicted shape. This is not unlike the consequences of the Marxist philosophy of the "inevitability of history." One believes that this is how things *must* happen, and one then uses violent or otherwise improper means to bring about that course of events; it is like Macbeth, fulfilling the witches' prophecies he "knows" to be true. But (a) there is no "inevitable" pattern knowable to us in history[44]—history is what people make of it—and (b) the inevitability, if there were such, of the end, does not constitute justification for the means of attaining it.[45]

In my view, it is necessary to distinguish between the state of Israel viewed in the context of international relations and the state as viewed in a religious context. So far as the former is concerned, the state should be regarded like any other, no abnormal "justification" sought for its existence, no double standards applied. As to the religious context, this is primarily an internal matter for the Jewish religion, in terms of which the return to the land may well be viewed as fulfillment of prophecy, though this will not be the only perspective from which it can be viewed even by Jews, and in any case the idea of fulfillment should be a general one, not a detailed "proof-text" analysis. There is also the subtle question of whether and to what extent the modern concept of the nation state corresponds to anything envisaged by the prophets or other pre-modern Jewish thinkers.

However, for Jews to demand that people of other religions acknowledge the Return as a fulfillment of prophecy is misguided;[46] it is tantamount to demanding that others accept a specifically Jewish theological outlook, and such a demand is in essence triumphalist. There may indeed be others—some fundamentalist Christian groups, for instance—who see the Return as a fulfillment of prophecy, but it is not a necessary part of Christian theology to read prophecy in this way, and it is not for Jews to demand of Christians that it be so. Moreover, when Christians *do* read scripture in this literal fashion, they read the New Testament as well, and are likely to see the return in a context which does not please Jews at all.[47]

5. Eschatology—Jewish and Christian

If by eschatology we refer to trito-Isaiah's concept of "new heavens and a new earth" (Is 66:22), then, of course, there are many Jews of traditional outlook whose ultimate expectations are of this nature. Since it is difficult to relate this belief to the actual state of Israel, or indeed to any clearly conceivable state, such people regard the present state as a non-prophetic political entity or as the "beginning of redemption."

For myself, I find such eschatological ideas too hard to grasp. The modern scientific cultural revolution and the British empirical tradition in which I was nurtured lead me to admit that I find old-fashioned eschatological talk no more than a hazy way of offering hope that one day things will be better. Part of the trouble is that whereas the ancients, both Jewish and Christian, were thinking of a rather short time for life on earth—say six thousand years, ending with a grand millennium—I have to contemplate a possible future for humanity in terms of billions of years. Scale alters perspective. I also have quite different notions from the ancients of how people function, even of the "body/soul" relationship. It certainly seems less than satisfactory to offer a "solution" to the human problem in terms of a radical change to the substance of earth and sky.

As to Jewish attitudes to specifically Christian eschatology, one can only say that as Jews reject the idea of incarnation there can be no centrality for a new appearance of Christ. Needless to say, the visions of the book of Revelation make little sense in Jewish terms either.

If, however, we take a more modernist view of eschatology, along the lines to which I have indicated my own commitment, some rapprochement between Jews and Christians becomes possible. After all, both groups look forward to a kingdom of God on earth. Though we may believe that only with God's grace and in God's own time it will actually come about, the improvements in social structures and relationships we believe it will consolidate are something toward which we can already labor. To a large extent we can do this together, for we share many common ideals. Still, we should not do it exclusively, but together with others of good will, even if they are "neither Jew nor Greek." In all honesty, none of us can conceive the "final" parousia. Why try? We will only quarrel. Far better to sink our quarrels and engage in the work we are here to do.

V. JEWISH-CHRISTIAN DIALOGUE TODAY

1. Opportunities

In its broadest sense, the Jewish-Christian dialogue is but part of a dialogue of all faiths and peoples. This offers new and unprecedented opportunities to the faiths of the world. Until now they have squandered much of their energy in quarreling with each other or among themselves, or in attempts at world domination by missionizing. Now they can learn to work together for the welfare of the planet and all who share it.

Jewish-Christian dialogue took root in the common battle against racial prejudice, whether in the American civil rights movement, or in response to Nazism. A recent instance of similar joint concern was evidenced at the 1987 Anglican-Jewish Consultation, where the themes on which discussion focused were AIDS and the problems of Britain's Inner City Areas of Deprivation.[48] Thus there is a continuing opportunity and need to pool resources, spiritual and material, to work together for social welfare.

Considerable areas of disagreement exist among religious people, for instance on abortion and a host of other medical problems. Yet, as the same Anglican-Jewish Consultation showed, the differences are not broadly between the two faiths, but rather between liberals and conservatives in each. This suggests that there is room for common discussion on such matters.

The opportunity must be seized by Christians and Jews together to relearn, even to rewrite, their history, in the light of modern scholarship.

Guilt must be recognized and confessed and reconciliation pursued. But reconciliation must not be too lightly conceded, lest the deep errors of the past not be faced. The healing process cannot be forced, and it will be both slow and painful.

Together, Jews and Christians should face the great problems posed by the modern worldview to traditional forms of both faiths. What do archaeology and biblical criticism mean in terms of the authority we vest in the text or meaning of scripture? The Genesis/evolution debate is *not* a specifically Jewish or Christian problem, but a shared Jewish *and* Christian one. Do we yet have the courage and self-confidence to face this and similar questions together?

Let us by all means share in the reassessment of our common heritage in the face of new notions of time, space and historical development, of man's place in nature, and of society and its units and relationships.

Not least of the intellectual challenges we face is the series of problems arising from the philosophical critique of religious language. The question to ask, in the first instance, is not "Do we believe in God?" but "What are we saying when we talk about God?"

2. Problems

Dialogue is sometimes inhibited because of the difficulty of embracing both points of view at the same time. Such theoretical or theological difficulties are by no means fatal to dialogue, for dialogue is between people, not theories, and people who are willing can find ways to be enriched by each other, notwithstanding fundamental disagreements. Once again, it is necessary to stress the role of the philosophy of language in enabling us to climb out of the individual, restrictive frameworks of our traditions and together explore the full range.

Sometimes dialogue is inhibited by actions which undermine people's confidence and trust. Missionizing and politicization are in this category.

(a) Theoretical Difficulties

There is a theological gulf, particularly with regard to the centrality and divinity of Christ, which is not bridgeable by traditional theological means. The more liberal theologians on both sides may be able to reach an accommodation; for instance, any Christian theology which sees talk and stories about Jesus as a paradigm of reality rather than as factual propositions about unique events is accessible to those Jews whose theology is similarly reductionist.

Radical theological revision may be required, and great courage is needed for this. Christian scholars have often attained this, revising their Christology in the light of the new understanding of Jews and Judaism. The onus for such revision lies more heavily on Christians than on Jews. True, Jews have made harsh statements about Christians and have misunderstood Christianity, and they must abandon such positions. But there is no way in which Judaism has ever defined itself at the expense of Christianity, as its true fulfillment, or as the replacement of villainous Christians; conversely, Christians have classically defined themselves in terms of the rejection/fulfillment of Judaism and the replacement of the Jewish people.

Jews and Christians share the basic concept of mission and much of its content. However, the more christological (in a doctrinal sense) as opposed to ethical and spiritual the Christian mission becomes, the more it conflicts with the Jewish mission instead of harmonizing with it. Clearly, much intellectual work has to be done here on both sides.

(b) Practical Difficulties

Missionizing undermines confidence and trust. If Christians target Jews in their "missions," there will be no dialogue; Christians will be talking to themselves, for no Jew will willingly stay to listen. This is not to say that Christians will not "witness to Christ" in dialogue as elsewhere; those who take part in dialogue are "witnesses" to that in which they believe. But they will not proselytize. Indeed, one of the remarkable advances in recent years has been the abandonment by most major western church bodies of active proselytizing of Jews. There are anomalies of course, one of these being the Church's Ministry amongst the Jews (previously the Church's Mission to the Jews) which operates under the umbrella of the Church of England. One would like to see this organization make a similar volte-face to that of the Roman Catholic Order of Sion, whose sisters have turned the original proselytizing aspirations of the order on their head, have won the confidence of the Jewish people, and are making an invaluable contribution to the development of Christian Jewish relations.[49]

I would not like to suggest a parallel between Jewish campaigns on behalf of Israel and Christian missionizing. It is certainly right and proper that Israel should figure on the dialogue agenda, and noteworthy that this principle has at last been accepted by the Vatican in the dialogues of its Liaison Committee with the International Jewish Committee on Interreligious Consultations. It must consistently be made clear by Jews that anything which is perceived as hostility toward Israel (rather than legitimate criticism) undermines trust and risks rendering dialogue impossible. However, it is improper to make demands of the dialogue partner. Arthur Hertzberg certainly went too far[50] in demanding that the Holy See extend full diplomatic recognition to Israel. I agree that it ought to. But that is not the point. As John M. Oesterreicher observed,[51] "Headlines often mislead, but 'Rome Must Recognize Israel' renders exactly the opinion Rabbi Arthur Hertzberg expresses. . . . I am surprised that he would deem dialogue possible when one partner makes demands regarding its nature and outcome."

In sum, there must be sensitivity to each other's fears and concerns, and a careful guarding of the conditions which allow trust.

Religion is a strange and potent thing. People that I played with, went to school with, share a whole language and culture with, in the marketplace, the concert hall, the laboratory, at the hustings, on the street, in all the facets of everyday life—we don't have to handle each other with kid gloves. But dress us up as theologians, professing the love of God and man and the pursuit of peace, and put us in the conference hall labeled as Jews and Christians, and we hardly know each other, we are nervous, we tread softly lest we unleash hatreds and suspicions. Is this the cost of spirituality?

3. The Way Ahead—Education

How do we move from pious resolutions to a changed society?

A vast educational task lies ahead, for the roots of hatred are not only deep but sacred, and the poison has spread to the language, images and stereotypes of western culture even where it is no longer Christian. Attitudes persist beyond the theologies that generated—or perhaps merely justified—them.

So while scholars and theologians talk, their best ideas must find their way into the classrooms of our seminaries, universities, and teacher training colleges, and, through the newly trained clergy and teachers, inspire young minds to create a new and peaceful culture and society for the generations to come.

NOTES

1. "Natural language" is the term used to indicate such languages as English, French, and Hebrew which have evolved "naturally" rather than been created to serve specific purposes.

2. That some terms are given in Hebrew does not imply that the others should be understood as in a Christian context. Each term must be understood within a context which the others help to define. The Hebrew terms are: *Torah*—in a narrow sense, the first five books of scripture; more broadly, the sum total of God's revelation in its impact on human life. *Mitzva*—commandment, the specific expression of God's will, as in "Love your neighbor as yourself" (Lv 19:18), or "Remember the sabbath day" (Ex 20:8). *Teshuva*—returning to God, penitence. *Tefilla*—prayer. *Tsedaka*—charity. *Hesed*—love, kindness, compassion. *Yetser*

tov—the good tendency within each soul, in conflict with the bad tendency (*yetser ra*).

3. I have explored the question of religious use of language in, "The Language of Dialogue in World Religions," in *World Faiths Insight* (Journal of the World Congress of Faiths), 1987.

4. Dan Jacobson, *The Story of the Stories* (London: Secker & Warburg, 1982), esp. chapter 4.

5. J.B. Agus, "The Covenant Concept," in *Journal of Ecumenical Studies,* Spring 1981. I cite from the version in *Christian Jewish Relations,* March 1982, p. 7.

6. Ibid. p. 8.

7. Ibid. p. 9.

8. This is referred to in many places in rabbinic literature, amongst them T.B. *Yoma* 28b.

9. Moses Maimonides (1135–1204), in his vast *Guide for the Perplexed,* uses the term only twice, so far as I can tell (3:30 and 3:32), and in both cases only incidentally.

10. T.B. *Nedarim* 31b.

11. T.B. *Sanhedrin* 44a.

12. Judah Halevi, *Kuzari* (New York: Schocken, 1964²), trans. H. Hirschfeld, 5:23. See also 4:23. See the end of Maimonides' *Mishneh Torah* for one of his clearest statements of the historical role of Christians and Muslims in familiarizing the nations with the ideas of God and scripture.

13. T.B. *Sanhedrin* 56. Some sages extend the list. The best modern account of the Noahide commandments is David Novak's "The Image of the Non-Jew in Judaism," in *Toronto Studies in Theology* (Edwin Mellen Press), 1983, vol. 14.

14. David Hartman, "On the Possibilities of Religious Pluralism from a Jewish Point of View," in *Immanuel* (Jerusalem), Summer 1983, no. 16.

15. Diogenes Laertius 1:33. See Martin Hengel, *Jews, Greeks and Barbarians* (London: SCM, 1980), p. 78, for an exploration of the idea of racial superiority in the Hellenistic world.

16. This translation is based upon *Yalkut Shimoni* on Judges 5. See also *Tosefta Berakhot* 7:18, T.J. *Berakhot* 9:2 and T.B. *Menahot* 43b.

17. I have in mind Gerald O'Collins' contribution to the symposium "Salvation and Redemption in Judaism and Christianity," in *Face to Face* (New York), Spring 1988, vol. xiv, p. 18.

18. Following Jerome's questionable translation of Romans 5:12 as in *quo omnes peccaverunt.*

19. *Stromateis* 3, 16, 100.

20. Isaac Luria (1534–1572), known as Ari Haqadosh ("the holy lion") from the initial letters of his name, was the most influential of the Safed mystics.

21. Gershom Scholem, *The Messianic Idea in Judaism* (New York: Schocken, 1974³), p. 43.

22. For instance, T.B. *Megilla* 29a: "Rabbi Simon the son of Yohai taught:

'See how beloved in Israel . . . for wherever they were exiled the Shekhinah (divine Presence) accompanied them into exile. . . .' " To some extent this is a rejoinder to Christian talk about the rejection of Israel by God.

23. Cf. Abraham J. Heschel, *The Prophets* (1971), vol. 2, chap. 4. Heschel contrasts this standpoint with that of the doctrine of the impassivity of God as adumbrated by the church fathers in their conflict with the Marcionites. It does not seem to occur to Heschel that in Christianity the impassivity of the Father is balanced by the extreme pathos of the Son.

24. An account of Luria's theory of creation may be found in Gershom Scholem, *Major Trends in Jewish Mysticism* (Jerusalem: Schocken, 1941), Lecture 7.

25. T.B. *Kiddushin* 30b. Unattributed.

26. *Tosefta Sanhedrin* 13.

27. *Mishnah Sanhedrin* 10:1.

28. Emil Fackenheim, in *To Mend the World*, strongly espouses this view.

29. Adolf Hitler, *Mein Kampf*, end of chapter 2.

30. English Christians, I am ashamed to say. Although Josephus in *Contra Apionem*, rebuts a similar accusation, the first recorded use of this base fabrication by Christians was at Norwich in 1144.

31. See *Luther, Lutheranism and the Jews*, eds. Jean Halperin and Arne Sovik (Geneva: Lutheran World Federation, 1984). This is a report of the Second Consultation between representatives of the International Jewish Committee for Interreligious Consultations and the Lutheran World Federation; the Consultation took place in 1983, the five hundredth anniversary of Luther's birth. The Lutheran participants made the courageous statement: "We Lutherans take our name and much of our understanding of Christianity from Martin Luther. But we cannot accept or condone the violent verbal attacks that the Reformer made against the Jews . . . we believe that a christological reading of the Scriptures does not lead to anti-Judaism, let alone antisemitism" (ibid. p. 9).

32. See section V. below.

33. Op. cit. p. 279.

34. Ibid. p. 282.

35. A. Roy Eckardt, *Jews and Christians: The Contemporary Meeting* (Bloomington: Indiana University Press, 1986), p. 16.

36. Ibid. chapter 8, headed "Along the Road of Good Intentions." The models are those of (1) Joseph E. Monti, (2) Ronald Goetz, (3) Paul van Buren, (4) J.-B. Metz and John Pawlikowski, and (5) Eckardt himself! In chapter 8 he offers tentatively "another road." Notwithstanding Eckardt's strictures, the works of Monti and the others are more than a starting point for the reconstruction of Christian thought after the Holocaust.

37. This was an interview in *Il Sabato*, October 24, 1987. Ratzinger subsequently said that the Italian text was misleading, and clarified his meaning in a letter to Cardinal Willebrands, who forwarded it to Christian and Jewish leaders in the United States after they had requested the clarification.

38. Justin Martyr, *Dialogue with Trypho.*

39. Jerome, Tract on *The Promised Land.*

40. Augustine, *Reply to Faustus the Manichean.*

41. See Gershon Greenberg, "Fundamentalists and Israel," in *Christian Jewish Relations* (London), September 1986, no. 19/3.

42. For Kook himself, of course, it was the *yishuv,* or Jewish settlement in Palestine; he died before the state was established.

43. "What death is worse for the soul than the liberty to err?" Augustine, *Epistola* 185—letter to Count Boniface in the year 417.

44. See K. Popper, *The Poverty of Historicism* (London: Routledge & Kegan Paul, 1957), for a devastating criticism of the concept of "laws of history."

45. On the abuse of scripture for political ends, see my paper "Political Implications of the Belief in Revelation," in *The Heythrop Journal* (London), 1984, no. xxv/2.

46. In *Christian Jewish Relations* 18/3, September 1985, p. 71, I argued along similar lines in support of paragraph 25 of the Vatican's (then) new document *The Common Bond,* which invited Christians to understand the Jewish religious attachment to the land while themselves envisaging the state of Israel and its political options "not in a perspective which is itself religious, but in their reference to the common principles of international law." Predictably but sadly, the document was attacked by many Jews precisely because it urged Catholics not to look on Israel as fulfillment of prophecy.

47. See Greenberg, loc. cit.

48. There is a short report of this Consultation in *Christian Jewish Relations,* Fall 1987, no. 20/3, p. 39.

49. For an account of the transformation of the Sisters of Sion see Charlotte Klein, "From Conversion to Dialogue," in *Christian Jewish Relations,* September 1982, No. 15/3.

50. In an article in *The New York Times,* December 4, 1985.

51. *Christian Jewish Relations.* March 1986, no. 19/1.

The Covenant as the Key: A Jewish Theology of Jewish-Christian Relations

Elliot N. Dorff

A. JEWISH AMBIVALENCE ABOUT THE COVENANT IDEA

Modern Jews are not used to describing themselves in the language of "covenant." In part that is because the word is not commonly used nowadays (except, perhaps, by lawyers), and hence it is not a word or concept that comes easily to mind. Those who do think about it are often reticent to use it for one of several ideological reasons. Many Jews have difficulty associating with the ancient, biblical events of revelation in which the covenant between God and Israel was formed because they are uncomfortable with religion generally. Even religiously committed Jews hesitate to use the term because Christianity adopted it in claiming that there is a covenant which supersedes the old one. (The Hebrew words usually translated "New Testament" literally mean "new covenant.") Therefore, in order to avoid Christian associations and claims, Jewish leaders and laypeople for the last two thousand years have substituted other terms to express their Jewish commitment.

In the modern period, enlightenment ideology made Christians more willing to treat Jews as equals. Jews have wanted to be forthcoming in their response, and some have seen covenant terminology as an obstacle to mutual acceptance and interaction. In other words, before the enlightenment Jews avoided the term "covenant" for fear that it would encourage assimilation with Christians; after the enlightenment some Jews have had the opposite problem with the term, fearing the exclusivity that it involves. Either way, the word does not sit well with Jews, and it has not done so for a very long time.

Nevertheless, it is my contention that for Christians to understand Jews, and for Jews to understand themselves, both groups must confront the meaning and implications of the covenant idea. For better or for worse, that idea articulates the essence of Judaism more clearly than any other. It defines the nature and content of the relationship between God and the Jewish people; it provides the rationale for the authority and methodology of Jewish law; and it delineates the goals of Judaism—i.e. to make life holy in accordance with the model and command of God, our covenanted partner, and to work for the physical and moral improvement of life in preparation for messianic times.[1]

The covenant idea is crucial for the understanding, not only of Judaism, but also of Jews. It provides the primary assumptions by which Jews understand themselves. Even if modern Jews are less religious than their ancestors, it is no exaggeration to say that the covenant idea has shaped the mind and heart of the Jew from biblical times to the present. However uncomfortable some Jews may be with the concept when they think of it consciously, it is part of the very psyche of the Jew.

Clarity about the meaning and implications of the covenant idea is essential not only for Jewish self-understanding, but also for Christians' comprehension of Jews, for Jews' perceptions of Christians, and for the development of meaningful Jewish-Christian relations. Only a full-bodied grasp of Jews and Judaism can make for a realistic assessment of the Jewish partner in that relationship. Moreover, since Christianity developed out of a new interpretation of the biblical covenant, Christian perceptions of Jews and Judaism are deeply rooted in the covenant idea. Conversely, Jews' views of Christians grow out of the Jewish rejection of the new Christian covenant theology.

Because of the centrality of the covenant in these crucial matters of definition and relationship, I have devoted three previous articles to the theological and legal implications of the covenant idea for contemporary Jewish self-understanding.[2] In yet another article I examined and evaluated important efforts by two modern Jewish theologians to reshape the covenant idea to account for past and present relations with non-Jews.[3] In this essay, after first briefly pointing out some important features of the traditional covenant idea relevant to our topic, I shall articulate my own theology of the covenant which, I hope, can serve as a theological grounding for mutual understanding and for cooperative Jewish-Christian relations in the future.

B. THE TRADITIONAL COVENANT CONCEPT: NATIONALISM AND UNIVERSALISM

The national character of the covenant is clear-cut in both biblical and rabbinic literature. The covenant is specifically between God and the Jewish people; its terms do not apply to others:

> Now, then, if you will obey me faithfully and keep my covenant, you shall be my treasured possession among all the peoples. Indeed, all the earth is mine, but you shall be to me a kingdom of priests and a holy nation (Ex 19:5–6).

> I the Lord am your God who has set you apart from other peoples . . . you shall be holy to me, for I the Lord am holy, and I have set you apart from other peoples to be mine (Lev 20:24–26).[4]

The rabbis continued this theme. Probably the best indication of this is what they say with reference to the sabbath, which is the symbol of the ongoing covenant between God and Israel and consequently, according to the rabbis, the equivalent of all the other commandments.[5] The Bible says:

> The Israelite people shall keep the sabbath, observing the sabbath throughout the ages as a covenant for all time. It shall be a sign for all time between me and the people of Israel (Ex 31:16–17).

On this the rabbis comment:

> It [the Sabbath] is a sign between Me and you" (Exodus 31:17), that is, and not between Me and the other nations of the world (*Mekhilta,* Ki Tissa).

This was not simply a matter of ideology; it had a pervasive effect on practice as well. Specifically, Jewish law operates like any other legal system in assuming that its rights and obligations apply fully only to the members of the national group. The rabbis make this explicit by asserting that non-Jews are subject to only the seven commandments given to the children of Noah, i.e. prohibitions against murder, idolatry, incest, eating a limb torn from a living animal, blasphemy, and theft and the requirement to establish laws and courts.[6] Non-Jews were given certain protections and privileges in Jewish law,[7] as aliens often are in legal systems, but they were not required to take on "the yoke of the commandments" (a rabbinic expression) because that was exclusively a feature of God's covenantal relationship to the Jews.

That part of the Jewish covenantal notion is fairly easy for Christians to understand because Christianity also conceives itself as the prime way of relating to God—indeed, as the "new covenant." What is probably harder to communicate is the fact that for the Jewish tradition this did not mean, as it did for much of Christianity, that it was the only way in which people could fulfill God's will for mankind and be "saved" (a word which means something very different in Judaism than it does in Christianity). Jews are required to obey the law because they are part of God's covenant with Israel at Sinai;[8] non-Jews were never part of the Sinai covenant, and therefore they are not obligated under it. This does not mean, though, that they are excluded from God's concern or prevented from enjoying God's favor. On the contrary, if they abide by the seven commandments given to Noah and seek to be righteous, they have done all that God wants of them. "The pious and virtuous of all nations participate in eternal bliss," the rabbis said[9]—a sharp contrast to the eternal damnation inherited by those who reject Jesus according to some versions of Christianity. Even at the prime moment of nationalistic triumph, the exodus from Egypt, the rabbis picture the ministering angels singing songs of praise over the destruction of the Egyptians in the Red Sea, but God rebukes them, saying, "My children lie drowned in the sea, and you sing hymns of triumph?"[10] Thus covenant does not entail exclusivity or triumphalism in Judaism.

It is not easy, though, to balance a sense of appreciation and pride in being God's covenanted people and following God's preferred way with the firmly held belief that, as God's creatures, all people are the object of his concern and eligible for his favor. The tensions involved inevitably meant that sometimes one of these tenets was emphasized to the exclusion of the other, largely dependent upon the particular historical circumstances. Thus, during the Hadrianic persecutions, one understandably hears expressions of extreme antipathy, like that of Simeon bar Yohai that "The best of gentiles should be killed"; on the other hand, during the more friendly atmosphere of early Sassanid Babylon, Samuel claims that God makes no distinction between Israel and the nations on the day of judgment.[11] The balance that Judaism affirms, however, reasserted itself in other times and places.

Both the tensions and the balance are probably best illustrated in the Jewish notion of messianism. The ultimate aim, as the biblical prophet Isaiah declared, is that all people worship God so that there will be universal peace among people and in nature, even to the extent that the lion will lie down with the lamb.[12] But Israel has a special role to play as "a light of the nations,"[13] and, as several biblical prophets asserted, it is Israel's God that all people will ultimately worship and Israel's Torah that they will practice.[14] Moreover, according to the rabbis, in messianic times Jews will be rewarded for their efforts to make God's will known by the reunion of the tribes of Israel in the land of Israel, the rebuilding of Jerusalem, the restoration of Jewish political autonomy, and general prosperity—so much so that non-Jews will seek to convert to Judaism to take advantage of Jews' new status but will not be allowed to do so because their motive is not disinterested:

> "You brought a vine out of Egypt" (Psalms 80:8). As the vine is the lowliest of trees and yet rules over all the trees, so Israel is made to appear lowly in this world but will in the Hereafter inherit the world from end to end. As the vine is at first trodden under the foot but is afterwards brought upon the table of kings, so Israel is made to appear contemptible in this world . . . but in the Hereafter the Lord will set Israel on high, as it is said, "Kings shall be your nursing fathers" (Isaiah 49:23) (*Leviticus Rabbah* 36:2).

> In the Hereafter the gentile peoples will come to be made proselytes but will not be accepted (*B. Avodah Zarah* 3b).

Thus those who are part of God's covenant with Israel are to enjoy special privileges for the added covenantal responsibilities they have borne, but ultimately all people are to participate in the human fulfillment of messianic times and the hereafter.

The tension between national pride and universalist convictions which is evident in the biblical and rabbinic doctrine of the covenant is also manifest in modern treatments of the subject. Franz Rosenzweig and Martin Buber, for example, affirm both elements of the balance, but the first emphasizes the special character of Israel and the second stresses the universal aspirations of the covenant. In that sense the first is a "nationalist" and the second a "universalist."[15]

While one can understand these tendencies purely on the basis of conflicting human emotions and the historical circumstances in which they are evoked, there are also deep, theological convictions involved. These have become manifest in the contemporary Jewish attempt to understand and justify pluralism *within* the Jewish community.[16] Many of the same considerations, however, can be fruitfully applied, albeit with some modifications, to the interaction *between* Jews and Christians. In the following sections, then, I shall present, in turn, historical, epistemological, and theological grounds for a vibrant theological pluralism within Judaism, followed by an exploration of how these arguments might be employed in the Jewish-Christian encounter.

C. HISTORICAL AND PHILOSOPHICAL GROUNDS FOR JEWISH PLURALISM

All communities, including the Jewish one, develop organically. That is, like an organism, every community changes over time in response to both internal and external circumstances. No community can long endure if it does not do this, any more than an organism can.

A broad, historical perspective, then, should impart a degree of humility to those trying to set definite bounds on the ideology, practice, or even membership of a community and should make one somewhat less earnest in doing so. Even Moses, according to the Talmud, could not understand the Jewish tradition as expounded fourteen centuries later in the school of Rabbi Akiba.[17] Theoretical attempts to define communities are post facto rationalizations of what happens in a largely a-rational way, and one cannot establish limits on the ideology or practice of a community with any degree of confidence in their accuracy or durability.

This does not mean that communities, by nature, are temporary or incoherent. Quite the contrary, the metaphor of an organism is meant precisely to capture the continuity and integrity of communities as well as their ability to withstand and even foster change. Like organisms, living communities adapt to new circumstances by adjusting some of what they do and how they do it, but they retain their identity in the process. Communities *do* define themselves, even if it is always in an ongoing, organic, logically haphazard way.

Several factors enable them to do this. Groups of people are distinct and ongoing communities, despite change, because, in part, they share a history and its heroes; they also are aware of themselves and are perceived by others as a community; they work together as a community; and, finally, they have shared goals—a shared vision and mission. All the legal and intellectual attempts to define the limits and content of Jewish identity gain whatever degree of authority they have from this shared life.

While such efforts have built-in limitations, they are clearly worthwhile. Attempts to give communal life rational form can contribute immensely to the community's self-awareness and its plans for the future. Furthermore, each community has the *right* to define itself. One should simply not exaggerate the degree to which human beings can devise a communal definition fully adequate to ever-changing historical facts.

If we have difficulty putting the facts of human history in intelligible form, how much more do we realize our limits when it comes to discovering God and defining what God wants of us. That is, the historical grounds for epistemological humility are augmented by philosophical considerations. We are not, of course, totally at a loss in trying to know God; God has given us intellectual faculties and, for Jews, the Torah to guide us. But we each, as the rabbis recognized, will understand God and his will according to our own individual abilities and perspective.[18] "Every way of man is right in his own eyes, but the Lord weighs the hearts" (Prov 21.2); as Rashi, an important medieval Jewish commentator, explains, this means that God judges each of us by our intentions since a human being cannot be expected to know the truth as God knows it.

The effects of history on religion and the limits of what we can really know about God and what he wants of us can, in the hands of some, become the motivation for rigidity and insularity, and, in the hands of others, the grounds for flexibility and pluralism. Orthodox Jews tend either to ignore historical changes and the epistemological limits on our knowledge of God, or to view them with horror. In view especially of the wide range of Jewish thought and practice in contemporary times, the Orthodox generally have tried to gather the wagons in a circle, as it were, to defend against the outside world. This has meant increasing resistance to change and refusal even to hear, let alone weigh, conflicting claims to truth. The Orthodox have, in large measure, shunned dialogue with other segments of the Jewish community, let alone with non-Jews. Certainty cannot be threatened or compromised.

Conservative and Reform Jews, however, have recognized these historical and philosophical facts to be an argument for mutual toleration. We can and should stand up for what we believe, and we should educate our children and adults accordingly. At the same time, we must recognize that other Jews may be committed to the tradition, intelligent, and morally sensitive, and yet have a different way of understanding and practicing Judaism than we have. It may be difficult to combine an energetic commitment to Judaism as we understand it with an openness to the interpretations of others, but the features of human history and epistemology discussed above leave us no rational alternative.

D. THEOLOGY: GOD WANTS PLURALISM

Commitment to pluralism, for Jews, should be motivated not only by the reality of historical change and the limitations of our knowledge, but also by Jewish theology. Rabbi Simon Greenberg (1901–   ), a contemporary Conservative rabbi, has pointed out some features of Jewish theology which warrant pluralism, and I will mention others.

Rabbi Greenberg defines pluralism as "the ability to say that 'your ideas are spiritually and ethically as valid—that is, as capable of being justified, supported, and defended—as mine' and yet remain firmly committed to your own ideas and practices."[19] But what bestows legitimacy upon varying views such that a person should be pluralistic in outlook? Political pluralism, as mandated in the American Bill of Rights, can be justified by pragmatic considerations, as James Madison does; the state needs to accommodate differing beliefs in order to promote the peace and welfare of its citizens. What, however, legitimizes a spiritual or ethical pluralism?

Greenberg says that he knows of no philosophic justification for pluralism, for that would entail the legitimation of accepting a position and its contrary or contradictory. There is, however, a religious justification: God *intended* that we all think differently.

Greenberg learns this from, among other sources, the Mishnah, the central collection of rabbinic law from the first and second centuries. Why, the Mishnah asks, did God initiate the human species by creating only one man? One reason, the Mishnah suggests, is to impress upon us the greatness of the Holy One, blessed be He, for when human beings mint coins, they all come out the same, but God made one mold (Adam) and yet no human being looks exactly like another. This physical pluralism is matched by an intellectual pluralism for which, the rabbis say, God is to be blessed: "When one sees a crowd of people, one is to say, 'Blessed is the Master of mysteries,' for just as their faces are not alike, so are their thoughts not alike."

The Midrash, the written record of rabbinic lore, supports this further. It says that when Moses was about to die, he said to the Lord: "Master of the Universe, You know the opinions of everyone, and that there are no two among Your children who think alike. I beg of You that after I die, when You appoint a leader for them, appoint one who will bear with (accept, *sovel*) each one of them as he thinks (on his own terms, *lefi da'ato*)." We know that Moses said this, the rabbis claim, because Moses describes God as "God of the *ruhot* (spirits [in the plural]) of all flesh" (Num 24:16).[20] Thus God *wants* pluralism so that people will constantly be reminded of his grandeur.

In addition to these sources mentioned by Greenberg, other elements of the tradition would also support a pluralistic attitude. God intentionally, according to the rabbis, reveals only a part of His truth in the torah, and the rest must come from study and debate.[21] Even with study there is a limit to human knowledge, for, as the medieval Jewish philosopher, Joseph Albo, said, "If I knew Him, I would be He."[22]

God as understood in the Jewish tradition thus wants pluralism not only to demonstrate his grandeur in creating humanity with diversity, but also to force human beings to realize their epistemological creatureliness, the limits of human knowledge in comparison to that of God. One is commanded to study; one *is* supposed to be committed to learning as much of God, his world, and his will as possible. But one must recognize that a passion for truth does not mean that one has full or exclusive possession of it; indeed, both of those are humanly impossible.

Moreover, one should understand that everyone's quest for religious knowledge is aided by discussion with others, for different views force all concerned to evaluate and refine their positions. The paradigmatic disputants, the school of Hillel, reverse their position a number of times in the Talmud, in contrast to the school of Shammai, which did so at most once. The Hillelites understood the epistemological and theological value of plural views and the need to learn from others.

Thus an appropriate degree of religious humility would lead one to engage in spirited, spiritual argumentation; one would not assume that one knows the truth and attempt to exclude others by fiat or by social pressure. One can and must take stands, but one should do so while remaining open to being convinced to the contrary. One should also recognize that others may intelligently, morally, and theologically both think and act differently. From the standpoint of piety, pluralism emerges not from relativism, but from a deeply held and aptly humble monotheism.

These sources indicate that pluralism is a divine creation; as such, human beings should try to imitate it, but they have difficulty doing so. To achieve the ability to be pluralistic is, in fact, the ultimate ethical and spiritual challenge, according to Greenberg. Just as "love your neighbor as yourself"—which, for Rabbi Akiba, is the underlying principle of all the commandments[23]—requires a person to go beyond biologically rooted self-love, pluralism requires a person to escape egocentricity. It is not possible for human beings totally to love their neighbors as themselves, and neither is it possible to be totally pluralistic. We are, by nature, too self-centered fully to achieve either goal.

The tradition, however, prescribes methods to bring us closer to these aims. Many of the biblical directions to gain love of neighbor appear in that same chapter 19 of Leviticus in which the commandment itself appears. The rabbis' instructions as to how to become pluralistic are contained, in part, in a famous talmudic source describing the debates of Hillel and Shammai: one must, like Hillel, be affable and humble and teach opinions opposed to one's own, citing them first.[24]

E. APPLYING THESE FACTORS TO OTHER FAITHS

It is difficult to convince some Jews of these historical, philosophical, and theological reasons to tolerate and, indeed, rejoice in plural views *within* the Jewish community. One can readily understand, then, that such Jews—largely within the Orthodox camp—would have even more difficulty applying this mentality to non-Jews. Moreover, most of the above sources were clearly intended only for intra-Jewish dialogue. Nevertheless, it seems to me that some of these same considerations can form the foundation for a mutually respectful interaction between Jews and Christians.

1. *History.* Historically, Christianity has been subject to change and redefinition at least as much as Judaism has, if not more. Even within the same denomination, creeds created centuries ago are continually changed, sometimes through outright amendment and sometimes through new interpretations, emphases, and/or applications. This constantly evolving nature of both Judaism and Christianity makes some of the faithful uneasy; they long for certainty and stability. At the same time, though, each religion retains its relevance and its dynamism only by opening itself to change.

In any case, whatever the pluses and minuses, the historical fact is that both religions *have* changed and continue to do so. The certainties of today, *even within the boundaries of one's own faith,* are not necessarily the convictions of tomorrow. History does not undermine one's ability to take a strong stand on what one believes, and it certainly does not prevent the contemporary Jewish community from authoritatively determining that groups like Jews for Jesus are decidedly *not* Jews. History does not totally undermine communal definitions and the coherence they bring. The historically evolutionary nature of both faiths should, however, help contemporary Jews and Christians get beyond the feeling that the present articulation of their faith is the only one possible for a decent person to have; on the contrary, history should teach us that people of intelligence, morality, and sensitivity most likely exist in other faiths too.

2. *Philosophy.* This realization is only reinforced when one turns from historical considerations to philosophical ones. All human beings, whatever their background or creed, suffer from the same limitations on human knowledge. Many of us have sacred texts and traditions which, for us, reveal God's nature and will as clearly and fully as we think possible. When we recognize that other peoples make the same claim, however, we must either resort to vacuous and disingenuous debates like those of the middle ages, or we must confront the fact that none of us can know God's nature or will with absolute certainty.

At the same time, just as the historical considerations do not make a specific faith impossible or inadvisable, so the philosophical factors do not. We may think that our particular understanding of God is the correct one for all people, *as far as we can tell,* and we may advance arguments toward convincing others of this, even though we know ahead of time that no human argument on these matters can be conclusive.

Alternatively, we may take a more "live and let live" approach, recognizing that part of the reason that the arguments for my faith seem most persuasive to me is because it is, after all, *my* faith and that of my family and my people. One need not deny cognitive meaning to religion to take such a position, as A.J. Ayer, R.B. Braithwaite, and others did in the middle of this century;[25] one need only be humble enough to recognize that none of us is an objective observer, that we all view the world from one or another vantage point, and that our autobiographical backgrounds inevitably do, and perhaps should, play a role in which viewpoint is ours. One could be, in Van Harvey's terminology, a "soft perspectivist" rather than a "hard perspectivist" or a "non-perspectivist": that is, one can say that we each have a perspective which influences how we think and act, that we do not look at the world through epistemologically transparent eyeglasses (vs. non-perspectivism), but one can allow that one's perspective does not need to blind a person to other perspectives (vs. hard perspectivism), that, indeed, one can possibly learn from the views of others.[26]

The latter of these approaches would, of course, make for a much stronger foundation for mutually respectful, Jewish-Christian relations, but even the former view, with its open recognition of the limits on what anyone can know of God, holds promise. That is because both come out of a philosophically accurate assessment of our knowledge of God: we can and do say some things about God and act on our convictions, and our beliefs and actions can be justified by reasons which can be shared and appreciated by others; but other, equally rational, moral, and sensitive people might differ with us and might have good reasons for what they say and do too. This is the result to be expected in areas where our knowledge is, by the very nature of the knower and the subject to be known, incomplete.

3. *Theology.* How would the theological considerations mentioned above apply to a Jewish understanding of Christians? In some ways, quite straightforwardly. If no two Israelites think alike, how much the more so do people from different backgrounds vary in their thoughts. If God is to be blessed for the former, he certainly should be blessed for the latter as well.

Furthermore, as master of the spirits of all flesh, God could clearly have created us to think alike. The fact that he did not do this underscores God's intention that we vary in our beliefs. As we have seen, the rabbis already drew one significant implication from this and from the restriction of Israel's covenant to the Israelites: non-Jews can attain salvation (however understood) outside the bounds of Jewish law.

Finally, it definitely is just as hard—if not harder—to extend one's empathy and sympathy not only to those within one's own group, but also to those with different affiliations, backgrounds, patterns of living, and aims. One needs all of the qualities ascribed to Hillel, and more. To act in this way surely partakes of the divine.

And yet there are some limitations to this line of reasoning as the basis for Jewish-Christian relations. It may be the case that God wants us to think independently, but ultimately the biblical prophets assert that Judaism's Torah is God's true teaching, the one which all nations will ultimately learn.

One should note that Micah, a younger contemporary of Isaiah, copies the latter's messianic vision but then adds a line of his own which effectively changes it: "Though all the peoples walk each in the names of its gods, we will walk in the name of the Lord our God forever and ever."[27] This is a decidedly pluralistic vision of messianic times: every people shall continue to follow its own god. Even so, Micah added this line *after* quoting Isaiah's vision that "the many peoples shall go and say: 'Come, let us go up to the mount of the Lord, to the house of the God of Jacob, that he may instruct us in his ways, and that we may walk in his paths.' For instruction shall come forth from Zion, the word of the Lord from Jerusalem" (Is 2:3; Mi 4:2). Thus even for Micah, apparently, other gods and other visions of the good life might exist, but it is only Israel which has the true understanding of God's will.

Thus God may indeed want multiple conceptions of the divine, as Greenberg maintains, but traditional sources assign non-Jewish views to a clearly secondary status. God may like variety among his creatures, and he may even hold people responsible only for what they could be expected to know (the seven Noahide laws); but ultimately only the Jews know what is objectively correct. This is liberal toleration—and it should be appreciated as such—but it certainly is not a validation of others' views. In that sense, it falls short of Greenberg's criterion that "your ideas are spiritually and ethically as valid—that is, as capable of being justified, supported, and defended—as mine." And, indeed, Greenberg himself may not have wanted to extend his thesis beyond disagreements among Jews.

I would take a somewhat broader view. It is only natural that Jewish sources cited in section B should reflect a tension between nationalism and universalism. God is, according to Jewish belief, the God of all creatures, but, at the same time, he chose the Jews to exemplify the standards he really wants for human life. This is how *Jews* understand God's will, the reason why Jews commit all their energies and, indeed, their very lives to Jewish belief and practice.

Despite this nationalistic side of the Jewish tradition, however, what ultimately rings through it is the rabbis' assertion that non-Jews fully meet God's expectations by abiding by the seven Noahide laws and the rabbis' statement that "The pious and virtuous of all nations participate in eternal bliss." Jewish sources, then, which speak about God wanting plural approaches to him within the Jewish community can apparently be applied, without too much tampering, to inter-communal relations as well. Of course, the same segments of the Jewish community which have difficulty with the former would undoubtedly have difficulty with the latter, but even some pluralists within the Jewish community would need to stretch their understanding and sensitivity to apply Jewish theology in this way. Nevertheless, a firm basis for this kind of theology exists within the Jewish tradition.

F. RECIPROCAL, CHRISTIAN RECOGNITION OF THE THEOLOGICAL VALIDITY OF JUDAISM

If Jews are to stretch in this way, they justifiably can expect Christians to do likewise. I personally have no doubt that Christians *can* find the requisite sources within their own tradition to do this, *if they choose to do so.*

Historically, of course, that has certainly not been the choice of most Christians. They have instead seen Christianity as the sole road to God. As a result, Christians have at best tolerated the continued existence of Judaism and Jews within their midst, and, more often than not, actively persecuted Jews for not converting to Christianity.[28]

Nevertheless, since the 1960s, there have been significant moves away from this dangerous teaching of contempt. Since the Catholic Church is, by far, the most populous Christian denomination, and since its opening to the Jews in 1965 stimulated many other Christian groups to follow suit, I will use their efforts in this regard to illustrate this point. As we shall see, despite significant movement by the Catholic Church within the last twenty-five years toward mutually respectful relations between Catholics and Jews, so far the Catholic Church has stopped short of validating the Jewish experience as a mode of salvation for Jews.

Nostra Aetate (1965), which broke open a new, salutary spirit in Catholic-Jewish relations, recognizes Judaism as the historical root of Christianity, but it does not describe it as a distinct religion with a substance and mission of its own. The *Guidelines,* published by the Vatican in 1974 to implement *Nostra Aetate,* moved to correct this: "Christians . . . must strive to learn by what essential traits the Jews define themselves in the light of their own religious experience." Paragraphs 2 and 3 of the official Vatican *Notes* to the *Guidelines,* published in 1985, require Catholics to study Judaism in a way which is not "occasional and marginal" but rather essentially and organically integrated in catechesis, and the Judaism they are to study is not only the religion of the Bible but "the faith and religious life of the Jewish people as they are professed and practiced still today."[29]

Subsequent paragraphs of *Notes,* however, make it clear that while Christians are to *study* Judaism as it is practiced by Jews, they are not to ascribe it divine legitimacy as a way to salvation for Jews; they are not, in other words, to assume that God continues to want Judaism to be practiced. The most distressing and exasperating section of *Notes,* then, especially after all this time in dialogue, is the following:

> 7. "In virtue of the divine mission, the Church" which is to be "the all-embracing means of salvation" in which *alone* [my italics] "the fullness of the means of salvation can be obtained" (*Unitatis Redintegratio,* 3) "must of her nature proclaim Jesus Christ to the world" (cf. *Guidelines,* I). . . .
>
> Jesus affirms (Jn 10:16) that "there shall be one flock and one shepherd." The Church and Judaism cannot then be seen as two parallel ways of salvation, and the Church must witness to Christ as the Redeemer for all, "while maintaining the strictest respect for religious liberty in line with the teaching of the Second Vatican Council" (Declaration *Dignitatis Humanae*) (*Guidelines,* I).

I certainly understand that Christians neither can nor want to abandon the texts of their tradition, and I would not ask them to do so. In contrast to fundamentalist Protestants, however, Jews and Catholics are keenly aware that the *meaning* of biblical texts and the very *choice* of which texts to emphasize and which to ignore are crucially shaped by the ongoing *tradition* of each faith. Unfortunately for both communities, the verse cited from the gospel of John has for centuries determined the way in which Christians have thought of Judaism. After the Second Vatican Council, Jews sincerely hoped that Catholics were moving beyond the triumphalism embedded in that verse. To do so would *not* require Christians to abandon their sacred texts; it would simply necessitate that they move away from focusing on John's perception of non-Christians and instead embrace and emphasize the many other elements of Christian tradition which recognize the legitimacy—and perhaps even the special vocation and aptness—of other people's faiths for them.

Indeed, the end of this very section alludes to how it might be done. The Second Vatican Council's *Declaration on Religious Liberty,* cited at the end of Section I, paragraph 7 of the *Notes,* and more extensively in paragraph 29F, clearly articulated a Catholic perspective; it was no less than the position of the most authoritative body in the church. I am not sure what theological resources in Catholic tradition motivated that statement. Perhaps it was the ultimate recognition that a loving and moral God can and does understand and appreciate the various ways in which human individuals and groups reach out to him. Whatever its basis, I would plead with Catholics that that statement of the Vatican Council shape the evolution of their tradition in our time so that they can move beyond the triumphalism in John and in paragraph 7 of the *Notes.*

A related matter concerns the relationship between the Hebrew Bible and Christian scriptures. *Guidelines* maintains that the Old Testament "retains its own perpetual value" and "has not been canceled by the later interpretation of the New Testament," but "the New Testament brings out the full meaning of the Old, while both Old and New illumine and explain each other." Similarly, *Notes* (paragraphs 9, 13, 17) argues for a typological interpretation of the Bible, designed "to show the unity of biblical revelation (Old Testament and New Testament) and of the divine plan," for "the definitive meaning of the election of Israel does not become clear except in the light of the complete fulfillment (Rom 9–11), and election in Jesus Christ is still better understood with reference to the announcement and the promise (cf. Heb 4:1–11)."

Jews relate to the Hebrew Bible in a similar way. For Jews, of course, it is the rabbinic tradition which is the fulfillment of the Hebrew Bible, not the New Testament. As Christians do with the New Testament, Jews consistently relate passages of rabbinic literature to biblical sources, and, conversely, they see biblical texts through the eyes of rabbinic interpretations of those texts. Although some medieval Jewish commentators distinguish on occasion between the plain meaning of a biblical passage and the rabbinic interpretation of it, by and large Jews have virtually identified the meaning of the Bible with the interpretations the rabbinic tradition gave it. In an oft-repeated passage, the rabbis maintained that "even what a learned student will say before his teacher in the future was already revealed to Moses at Sinai."[30] The continuation of the Bible in the words of the rabbis was so fundamental an assumption among Jews that, with the exception of Spinoza, it is only in this century that Jews even considered the possibility that biblical religion might have been different from its later development in rabbinic Judaism. In fact, it is only in the last fifty years or so that Jewish scholars have applied the tools of historical analysis to the Torah. Orthodox Jews still refuse to do so.

As a result, Jews can certainly understand the linkage which Christians affirm between the Hebrew Bible and their continuing tradition based upon it. We only want Christians to recognize that Christian scriptures and tradition are the continuation and fulfillment of the Hebrew Bible *for Christians.* Similarly, the four pairs of concepts which *Notes* (paragraph 5) wants to balance in reading the Bible—promise and fulfillment; continuity and newness; singularity and universality; uniqueness and exemplary nature—are unobjectionable to Jews if it is clear that Jews and Christians apply these principles differently. The "fulfillment" of the liberation and salvation of the exodus, for example, and its "newness" are, for Christians, preeminently Jesus, while for Jews it is the messianic era still to come. Until such time, the exodus and Sinai, as understood by the rabbinic tradition, continue to govern our vision of what is and ought to be.

As part of the rapprochement between Christians and Jews in our time, then, Jews want contemporary Christians to abandon the triumphalism and chauvinism of the past, both in their relationships with Jews and in their reading of the Bible. One important manifestation of doing this would be a shift in policy on missionizing among Jews. Jews can understand Christians' desire to spread their faith, and they certainly appreciate that *Guidelines* warned Catholics to "take care to live and spread their Christian faith while maintaining the strictest respect for religious liberty, in line with the teaching of the Second Vatican Council." However, because Jews represent less than half of one percent of the world's population and Catholics more than twenty-five percent, and because Jews lost one-third of their numbers in the Holocaust and face major demographic problems due to assimilation and intermarriage, Jews would hope that Catholic respect for Judaism and Jews would result in a policy of renouncing conversionary efforts among Jews altogether.

Jews do *not* expect Catholics to abandon their belief in Jesus as *their* way to salvation. Furthermore, the recognition of legitimacy which I am seeking is *mutual*. As we have seen, Jews have always believed that Judaism is really what God wants, that ultimately, in the words of Isaiah 2:3, all peoples will come to Jerusalem to learn the Torah from Israel. But for millennia Jews have understood that Jewish law is only incumbent upon Jews, that indeed it is the *Jewish* way to salvation, and that righteous people in other groups can attain salvation in their specific ways. This Jew hopes that Catholics—and Christians of the other denominations as well —are increasingly coming to the same realization.

G. A REALISTIC BUT OPEN MODEL
OF THE COVENANT FOR OUR TIMES

With these considerations as a background, we are now prepared to suggest some features of a contemporary version of the covenant which, on the one hand, is realistic in its understanding of the past and present of both the Jewish and Christian communities but, on the other hand, holds out promise for better mutual relations. Such an interpretation of the covenant would, I think, have the following elements:

1. *The role of individuals in the covenant.* Modern covenant notions all too often ignore the mode and method of modernism and the enlightenment philosophy which motivated it—i.e. that people exist as individuals first and as members of groups second. What was exclusively a philosophic doctrine in the seventeenth century gained political expression in this country in the eighteenth, through the Declaration of Independence, the Constitution, and the Bill of Rights; but it has taken the better part of the last two centuries for that ideology to become part of the thinking, customs, and daily life of a large number of Americans. This *has* happened, however: people are crossing group lines (whether they be racial, religious, ethnic, or whatever else) in their schooling, their jobs, their housing, and, most importantly, their friendships (even to the point of intergroup marriages). Whether this is good or bad, it is a fact which has a strong influence on the thinking and action of modern Jews and Christians. Consequently a covenant concept which translates and applies the meaning and import of Judaism or Christianity to the modern world must come to grips with the individualism of modernity.

Individualism has implications for the covenant both internally and externally, i.e. within each group and in the group's relations to outsiders. Internally it means that religious leaders will have to recognize that individual Christians and Jews will not automatically have loyalty to Christianity or Judaism just because they were born into those faiths. People do need community, and many do want to have a relationship with God, but they now increasingly feel free to shop around for the form of religious expression which is most meaningful to them. *As individuals* they choose whether to affirm the covenant, and, if so, how.[31] Consequently religious leaders have to redouble their efforts in communicating the message of their form of the covenant if they want to retain their adherents, and religious groups have to prepare themselves religiously and socially for integrating many converts into the fold—a process for which Jews are especially unprepared because of the traditional lack of missionizing and conversion in Judaism.

Externally, modern individualism means that both the Christian and the Jewish communities must recognize that members of each faith will vary widely in their conceptions and practices: there is no stereotypical Christian or Jew anymore. This feature of the modern religious landscape holds great promise for relationships among Jews and Christians in that there is now a much greater chance that members of each faith community can relate to those of the other as people and not as "card-carrying" members of a group. This hopefully will make people more aware that people with patterns of belief and practice different from their own have worth too.

2. *The role of the group and its traditions in the covenant.* However much we moderns are individuals, we also deeply need to be part of a group. The covenant speaks directly to this need because through being covenanted with God as a community, we are also covenanted with each other and with our ancestors and our descendants for all time. Part of the power of the covenant idea is precisely the rootedness in an historical community which it affords.

This means that no modern concept of covenant can safely ignore the past and present traditions of the group in both belief and practice. That is, the individualism which we feel and live must be balanced with the social associations and commitments which we also feel and live. A modern covenant concept must contain enough of the group feeling and traditions to make it recognizably Jewish or Christian.

3. *The role of universal ideals in the covenant.* Judaism and Christianity have both particularist and universalist strains in their literature,[32] and it is important that a modern conception of covenant not lose sight of the universalism in each tradition in its efforts to accommodate the need for individualism and nationalism. The biblical and rabbinic traditions achieved a *balance* of the national and universal; we must incorporate attention to the individual along with those two, giving proper emphasis to each of the three elements.

The universal aspect of the covenant has two manifestations, both of which are important to retain and develop. Universalism in our own day involves the recognition that God can and does relate to all people. The particular way in which God relates to each group may vary, and it is inevitable that people will feel that their own way is best, but this should not produce the conclusion that other ways are necessarily bad, ineffective, or unauthentic. It may well be that God wisely entered into different forms of relationship with different peoples to fit the traditions, talents, and sensitivities of each group. It may also be that God has planned different roles for each group. Franz Rosenzweig suggested that Jews model what God wants and that Christians carry the message to the Gentiles; the respective numbers of the Jewish and Christian communities and their respective policies on missionizing seems to support such a view. As Seymour Siegel has said:

> If this suggestion were to be accepted by Jew and Christian, it would be possible to open a new era of dialogue and mutual enlightenment. Christians would not denigrate Judaism by viewing it as a vestige, an anachronism of ancient times. They would cease their missionizing activities vis-à-vis Jews. For Jews, there would be a new recognition of the importance of Christianity, of its spiritual dimension and its task to bring the word of God to the far islands.[33]

The other aspect of covenantal universalism affects our hopes for the future. The biblical promise of a messianic time when there would be universal peace, prosperity, goodness, and fulfillment, when God's teaching will be put "into people's inmost being" so that everyone will heed him (Jer 31:33–34), and when, *mirabile dictu*, God shall even "reconcile fathers with sons and sons with their fathers" (Mal 3:24)—that biblical promise is a crucial element of the covenant concept which must be continually reinforced. Our viewpoints and associations are indispensable at this time in history, when we can do no better, but ultimately our goal is no less than a completely fulfilled human experience for all humanity. This goal-directedness puts our lives in a broader context, thereby making them much more meaningful: I am not struggling for naught because my actions can contribute to bringing about messianic times for all humanity. No wonder why this universalist lament has been part of the covenant idea from the start.

4. *The role of God in the covenant.* The covenant is not just the constitution of a group of people, but an agreement with God. It is the divine component of the covenant that gives it ultimate authority, that pushes us to expand the scope of the covenant to encompass all human beings, and that holds out plausible promise for a messianic future. God's participation in the covenant also provides a powerful rationale for human worth and an effective antidote to loneliness. If God, after all, seeks relations with human beings, we must be worthy of such association (at least potentially); and since every human being incorporates divine worth, each person can relate to God, even at the times when it is difficult to relate to other human beings. No interpretation of the covenant which leaves God out can plausibly claim to be Jewish or Christian.

The elements of the covenant described above give it its social import, and any modern view must incorporate all of them. This, of course, is easier said than done, for several of them do not sit well together. If the covenant is to speak to the individual, how can it reinforce group associations and traditions; and if it is to do that, how can it be open to all human beings? These are real tensions in the covenant idea, but it is good that the concept has those tensions because they are part of life as we know it.

It is because the covenant expresses reality and does not hide it that it is as valuable as it is both descriptively and prescriptively. Religious leaders and laypeople alike would consequently do well to explicate the covenant, apply it to their own times, and indeed live by it, for then we make it eternal, as God expressly desires. As the psalmist says:

> Stock of Abraham his servant,
> sons of Jacob his chosen one!
> He is the Lord, our God,
> his authority is over all the earth.

> Remember his covenant forever,
> his word of command for a thousand generations,
> the pact he made with Abraham,
> his oath to Isaac.

> He established it as a statute for Jacob,
> an everlasting covenant for Israel (Ps 105:6–10).

NOTES

In all of the following notes, I shall use these common notations for the classical rabbinic texts:

M. = Mishnah (edited c. 220 C.E.); T. = Tosefta (edited at about the same time); J. = Jerusalem (or Palestinian) Talmud (edited approximately 400 C.E.); B. = Babylonian Talmud (edited c. 500 C.E.).

1. The relative roles of God and mankind in bringing about messianic times is a matter of dispute in Jewish sources, but most hold that the messiah will come as a result of the combined efforts of God and mankind, and some assign humanity a very significant part in bringing about messianic times.

2. "Judaism as a Religious Legal System," *The Hasting's Law Journal* 29:1331–1360 (July 1978); "The Meaning of Covenant: A Contemporary Under-

standing," in *Issues in the Jewish-Christian Dialogue,* Helga Croner and Leon Klenicki, eds. (New York: Paulist Press [A Stimulus Book]), pp. 38–61; and "The Covenant: The Transcendent Thrust in Jewish Law," *The Jewish Law Annual* 7:68–96 (1988).

3. "The Covenant: How Jews Understand Themselves and Others," *Anglican Theological Review* 64:4 (October 1982), pp. 481–501.

4. Cf. also Ex 34:10; Lev 25:39–46; Deut 7:1–11; 10:12–22; 33:4; Jer 11:1–13.

5. Cf. *J. Nedarim* 38b; *Exodus Rabbah* 25:12.

6. *T. Avodah Zarah* 8:4; *B. Sanhedrin* 56a, 60a.

7. According to rabbinic law, this included giving charity to the non-Jewish poor and personal obligations like burying their dead, attending their funerals, eulogizing their deceased, and consoling their bereaved; cf. *M. Gittin* 5:8; *T. Gittin* 5:4–5; and my article, "Jewish Perspectives on the Poor," in *The Poor Among Us: Jewish Tradition and Social Policy* (no editor listed) (New York: The American Jewish Committee, 1986), pp. 21–55, esp. pp. 37, 39–40.

8. See, for example, Deut 7:9–11; *The Haggadah of Passover,* ed. Philip Birnbaum (New York: Hebrew Publishing Company, 1953), p. 95; ed. Rachel Anne Rabinowicz (New York: Rabbinical Assembly, 1982), pp. 66–67.

9. *Sifra* on Leviticus 19:18.

10. *B. Megillah* 10b.

11. Simeon bar Yohai's statement: *J. Kiddushin* 4:11 (66c). Samuel's statement: *J. Rosh Hashanah* 1:3 (57a). Cf. Daniel Sperber and Theodore Friedman, "Gentile," *Encyclopedia Judaica* 7:410–414. As Sperber points out, the Jew's attitude toward the Gentile was largely conditioned by the Gentile's attitude toward him (see, for example, *Esther Rabbah* 2:3). Moreover, to the extent that there was Jewish antipathy toward Gentiles, it was never based upon racial prejudice, but rather motivated by Gentiles' idolatry, moral laxity, cruelty to Jews, and rejection of the Torah.

12. Is 2:2–4, 11–12.

13. Is 49:1–6; 51:4.

14. Is 2:2–4; Zeph 2:11; 3:8–9; Zech 14:9.

15. See my article cited above in n. 4, esp. pp. 484–493.

16. For a summary of a number of such approaches, see my article "Pluralism," about to appear in *Jewish Concepts in Today's World,* ed. by Steven T. Katz and published by B'nai Brith.

17. *B. Menahot* 29b.

18. Cf. *Mekhilta,* Yitro, #9 (in an abbreviated version); *Exodus Rabbah* 5:9; 29:1; *Pesikta d'Rav Kahana,* "Bahodesh Hashlishi" (on Exodus 20:2), near end of Chapter 12 (ed. Mandelbaum, I:224); *Midrash Tanhuma,* Shemot, #22 (ed. S. Buber, II: 7b); Yitro, #17 (ed. S. Buber, II:40a–40b); *Pesikta Rabbati* 21.

19. Simon Greenberg, "Pluralism and Jewish Education," *Religious Education* (Winter 1986), p. 23. Cf. also p. 27, where he links pluralism to the absence of violence in transforming another person's opinion.

20. *Ibid.* pp. 24, 26. The Mishnah cited is *M. Sanhedrin* 4:5; the blessing cited

is in *B. Berakhot* 58a; and the Midrash cited is in *Midrash Tanhuma* on Numbers 24:16.

21. *J. Sanhedrin* 22a; *Midrash Tanhuma,* ed. Buber, Devarim, 1a; *Numbers Rabbah* 19:6. These sources are reprinted in their original Hebrew form and translated in my book, *Conservative Judaism: Our Ancestors to Our Descendants* (New York: United Synagogue Youth, 1977), pp. 87, 99.

22. Joseph Albo, *Sefer Ha-Ikkarim,* Part II, Chapter 30, Isaac Husik, trans. (Philadelphia: Jewish Publication Society of America, 1946), Vol. II, p. 206.

23. *Sifra* to Leviticus 19:18. Ben Azzai instead cites "This is the book of the generations of Adam . . . in the likeness of God He made him" (Gen 5:1)—a principle which extends love beyond Jews ("your neighbor") and ties it directly to God, whose image should be appreciated in every person.

24. *B. Eruvin* 13b.

25. The two non-perspectivists mentioned, A.J. Ayer and R.B. Braithwaite, share the view that religion does not make true or false assertions but rather motivates one emotionally, but the former thinker sees this as a major limitation on religion, while the latter thinks that this description is both accurate and fine. Cf. A.J. Ayer, *Language, Truth, and Logic* (London: Dover, 1936, 1946), pp. 114–120; R.B. Braithwaite, *An Empiricist's View of the Nature of Religious Belief,* The Eddington Memorial Lecture for 1955 (Cambridge: Cambridge University Press, 1955), reprinted in Ian T. Ramsey, ed. *Christian Ethics and Contemporary Philosophy* (New York: Macmillan, 1966), pp. 53–73.

26. For the terms, "hard" and "soft" perspectivism, cf. Van A. Harvey, *The Historian and the Believer* (New York: Macmillan, 1966), pp. 205–230; cf. also James Wm. McClendon, Jr., and James M. Smith, *Understanding Religious Convictions* (Notre Dame: University of Notre Dame Press, 1975), pp. 6–8.

It is interesting to note that even a medieval, hard-line anti-rationalist like Judah Halevi was open to considering the claims of other faiths and recognized that part of his inability to accept them stemmed from the fact that they were not *his* faiths, that he had not had personal experience with them; cf. his *Kuzari,* Book I, Sections 5, 6, 25, 63–65, 80–91 (reprinted in Section Three of *Three Jewish Philosophers,* ed. Isaak Heinemann [Philadelphia: Jewish Publication Society of America, 1960], pp. 31–32, 35, 37–38, 41–45).

27. Mic 4:5. Compare Mic 4:1–3 with Is 2:2–4.

28. Father Edward Flannery, *The Anguish of the Jews: Twenty-Three Centuries of Anti-Semitism* (New York: Macmillan, 1965; revised and updated (New York/Mahwah: Paulist Press [A Stimulus Book], 1985), is an extensive, and, indeed, a landmark presentation of the evidence by a Christian. Cf. also Rosemary Ruether, *Faith and Fratricide: The Theological Roots of Anti-Semitism* (New York: Seabury Press, 1974) for a more theological treatment of the subject by an important Christian theologian.

29. The full names of the latter two documents are, respectively, *Guidelines and Suggestions for Implementing the Conciliar Declaration 'Nostra Aetate' (n. 4),* published in December 1974, by the Vatican Commission for Religious Relations

with the Jews; and *Notes on the Correct Way To Present Jews and Judaism in Preaching and Catechesis in the Roman Catholic Church,* published by the same body in June 1985.

30. J. *Peah* 2:6 (17a); J. *Megillah* 4:1 (74d); J. *Hagigah* 1:8 (76d); *Leviticus Rabbah* 22:1; *Ecclesiastes Rabbah* 21:9.

31. I discuss this at some length in the context of training rabbinical students in my article, "Training Rabbis in the Land of the Free," in *The Seminary at 100,* eds. Nina Beth Cardin and David Wolf Silverman (New York: The Rabbinical Assembly and the Jewish Theological Seminary of America, 1987), pp. 11–28. The phenomenon, however, pervades the Jewish community, as I indicate there.

32. For a good survey of the Jewish material on this, see Jacob Agus, "The Covenant Concept—Particularistic, Pluralistic, or Futuristic?" *Journal of Ecumenical Studies* 18:217–230.

33. Seymour Siegel, "Covenants—Old and New," *Jewish Heritage* (Spring 1967), pp. 54–59. Rosenzweig's suggestion appears in his *The Star of Redemption,* trans. William W. Hallo (New York: Holt Rinehart, & Winston, 1971 [first published in 1921]), Part III, Books I and II; cf. esp. p. 166. I discuss his theory in my article cited in note 4 above, pp. 484–490. Unlike Rosenzweig, however, I would not want to build in a decidedly secondary status to Christianity's role.

The Judeo-Christian Dialogue in the Twentieth Century: The Jewish Response

Walter Jacob

It is a very long road from the medieval *Toldot Yeshu* to Borowitz's *Contemporary Christologies: A Jewish Response.* In the middle ages the relationship between Judaism and Christianity, although sometimes cordial on a personal level, was intensely hostile on the religious level. For Christians there was always the hope that Jews would convert. When this did not involve physical harassment or mandatory attendance at Christian services it expressed itself through polemical attacks which portrayed Judaism as evil. The medieval antisemitic literature is large. *Nostra Aetate* was inconceivable.

On the Jewish side it was usually not safe to react vigorously against these attacks. After all, Jews represented a tiny minority in Christian lands. Mostly the majority religion was simply ignored by us. Occasionally anti-Christian literature circulated underground, some of it produced in Islamic lands or in places where freedom of religion existed, as in sixteenth century Lithuania where Isaac Troki produced his *Hizuq Emunah,* a vigorous defense of Judaism through a Jewish interpretation of biblical verses. This literature was neither large nor did it play a significant role in Jewish intellectual life.

More important for our relationship to Christianity, throughout the middle ages was the changing *halakhic* attitude toward Christianity. By the eleventh and twelfth centuries it was clear that the old view of Christianity as idolatry was neither useful nor realistic. It represented a misunderstanding of Christianity and furthermore hindered economic relationships between Jews and Christians in northern Europe. Therefore, Rabenu Tam and his followers declared Christianity to be monotheistic but on a different level than Judaism. This adjustment enabled Jews to establish new relationships and to feel less hostile toward their environment. In the Islamic world, Maimonides, who witnessed no economic pressure, judged Christianity as monotheistic, but with grave reservations. He considered Islam more akin to Judaism. Rabenu Tam's attitudes became the accepted view, but as Christian hostility persisted, our attitude toward Christianity did not develop further until the eighteenth century—in other words, until Christian power waned and the modern secular world emerged.

As we view the Judeo-Christian dialogue, twenty-five years after *Nostra Aetate,* we can see that major strides have been made but they were built on a century and a half of effort which must be appreciated. We must remember the early tentative steps in the direction of dialogue and understand the reluctance of Jewish scholars even to approach this area.

When we see Moses Mendelssohn, at the end of the eighteenth century, begin to move in this direction, we realize that he did so only to avoid a public confrontation with the Christian scholar Lavater. As Mendelssohn was primarily engaged in obtaining equal rights for Jews, he did not wish to compromise that effort. It would have been irresponsible for him to engage in a public dispute. Yet, he could not stand by idly while Judaism was attacked and maligned, and so he engaged in some discussions and a mild disputation on various aspects of Christianity.

The subsequent European figures who emerged in this quest for understanding Christianity approached it in a variety of ways. Joseph Salvador (1796–1873) wrote the first modern Jewish life of Jesus. Elijah Benamozegh (1823–1900) emerged from the Italian Jewish community to present a modern Orthodox critique of Christianity which represented the first engagement of a traditional figure with Christianity and Christian thought.

Those who emerged on the German Jewish scene, Abraham Geiger (1810–1874), Samuel Hirsch (1815–1889), Salomon Formstecher (1808–1899), and Salomon Steinheim (1789–1866), discussed Christianity from a variety of points of view. Geiger's concern was primarily historical while the others engaged in philosophical confrontations which sought to defend Judaism against philosophical attacks by German Christian thinkers; they wished to provide a foundation for discussions. Despite their serious efforts and their desire to engage in scholarly debate the

Christian world ignored them and there was no response to their efforts. Hermann Cohen (1842–1918) later developed his neo-Kantian critique and appreciation of Christianity. He received no response from Christian circles. Matters were somewhat different in America where Isaac Mayer Wise, and to a lesser extent other Jewish figures, expressed themselves frankly on Christianity and Christian thought. In the United States it was possible to speak without fear. Furthermore the fragmented and often theologically disinterested Christianity of North America permitted personal friendships between rabbis and ministers. Wise and other American Jewish leaders therefore proceeded with far less caution than their European counterparts. They were also unencumbered by traditions or institutions. We should look at all of these efforts of the eighteenth and nineteenth centuries as foundations for the future but they attained nothing even remotely akin to inter-religious conversation.

At the turn of the twentieth century, different roads were taken in Europe and North America. The open nature of North American society led to boldness and a grass roots movement toward inter-religious dialogue. Liberal rabbis and liberal ministers shared pulpits, engaged in public conversation, and occasionally sponsored joint social welfare programs. As the decades went on, main-line religious bodies became involved. It took a very long time for the national conferences of various churches to change their theological attitudes toward Jews and Judaism. However, the grass roots movements were not inhibited by lack of national support. This friendship was met with considerable joy on the Jewish side and hundreds of pulpit exchanges took place. No effort, however, was made to place this into a theological or a *halakhic* framework. A certain hesitancy about the new relationship was felt and manifested itself in a number of ways, including criticism of Shalom Asch's novels which appeared too friendly to Christian themes. It was one thing to proclaim friendship, talk to each other, and move gently in this direction but another to declare a permanent change had taken place, particularly as doubts remained about the nature of the Christian welcome. How positive was it? Could one rely on it in times of crises?

In Europe matters proceeded along more academic lines. The power of the dominant churches had diminished. So Leo Baeck (1873–1956) engaged Christianity in a different manner. His first work *The Essence of Judaism* (1904) was a response to the great Christian theologian Harnack's *The Essence of Christianity* which was hostile to Judaism. Baeck's response followed the medieval pattern in one significant way. Although the title suggested a response and the work itself demonstrated the vigor of Judaism, it did not mention Christianity a single time. The response, therefore, was oblique, but at least an academic dialogue was underway.

Most of the essays in which Baeck concerned himself with Christianity were historical and expository. At first he sought a Jewish understanding of Christianity; later he wished to discover a road of reconciliation between the two religions, which both believed themselves to have the final answer and had stood face to face through nineteen centuries of history without thoroughly examining each other. "And the usual, and inevitable, result of any talk was an increase in the feeling, on the Christian side, of being uncompromisingly rejected by the Jew, and, on the Jewish side, of being forcibly summoned and violently accused by the Christian—let alone the fact of the restrictions and burdens imposed on the Jew, or on behalf of, the Church."[1] There had been times to keep silent, he felt, but this was an age for attempting to speak, and it would be very wrong not to fully utilize the present-day situation, which encouraged such discussion among all religions.

Leo Baeck's basic attitude toward Christianity is best expressed in his long polemic essay "Romantic Religion." In this piece he contrasted "classic" Judaism with "romantic" Christianity. The discussion was executed on a lofty philosophical level, but the tone remained polemic in the characterization of Christian thought: "Feeling is supposed to mean everything: this is the quintessence of romanticism. . . . Its danger, however, which it cannot escape is this: the all-important feeling culminates eventually in vacuity or in substitutes, or it freezes and becomes rigid. And before this happens, it follows a course which takes it either into sentimentality or into the phantastic; it dodges all reality, particularly that of the commandment, and takes refuge in passivity when confronted with the ethical task of the day. Empathy makes up for much and gives a freedom which is really a freedom from decision and independence from inner obligation."[2]

Many Jewish scholars before Baeck had pointed to the Jewish elements of the New Testament, but none had tried to actually reclaim the gospels as a Jewish book. Of course, this effort was also criticized. It was not acceptable to Mayer, who felt, with some justification, that Baeck had abstracted the most beautiful traditions of the gospels, claiming them for Judaism and discarding the rest.[3]

R. Mayer criticized Baeck here for having created a special person out of Jesus from whom the Christian characteristics had been removed. This presented an erroneous and oversimplified view of early Christian history. Nonetheless, Mayer admitted, the picture of Jesus that emerged was truer and more sympathetic than the one given by many Christian scholars.[4]

Leo Baeck's contribution to a Jewish understanding of Christianity was considerable. He and Claude G. Montefiore were pioneer workers in this field, which had been touched by only a few other serious Jewish scholarly efforts before the turn of the century. Baeck's analysis of the Jewish elements of early Christianity was to be followed by other students; it has led to a greater understanding of Christianity by Jews. His polemical critique of Christianity clearly demonstrated the position of Judaism in basic theological matters.

Although Leo Baeck's works might have found an echo in the Christian scholarly world, they did not until very late, despite Leo Baeck's leadership in Jewish communal life. No inter-religious discussion on a personal or academic level emerged. It was not only the inertia but also the rigidity of the German churches both Lutheran and Catholic which made such an effort difficult. Then, of course, came the Nazi years when this was not possible. When Leo Baeck at the very end of his life spent time in the United States, he discovered a more open Christianity which he appreciated. He felt that here "Inner voices will be heard. To each other Judaism and Christianity will be admonitions and warnings: Christianity becoming Judaism's conscience and Judaism Christianity's. That common ground, that common outlook, that common problem which they come to be aware of will call them to make a joint approach."[5]

Another European approach may be found in Claude G. Montefiore (1858–1938) who felt that liberal Judaism would permit discussion and friendship. He rejected much of Jewish nationalism and the halakhah. With these issues of the Judeo-Christian debate removed from the scene he wrote two works on the New Testament which approached the literature from a rabbinic point of view. He wrote on Jesus, Paul and much else as he sought to build bridges between the two religions. He rejected all Christologies and rearranged the life of Jesus to fit his own liberal Jewish views.

Jesus was never viewed as divine by Montefiore. "I would not deny that the dogma of the incarnation of God and Jesus has had its effects for good as well as evil. But nonetheless Liberal Jews do hold that it rests on a confusion, the confusion of a man with God."[6] We can never associate Jesus with the highest concepts as goodness, for they belong to God.[7] Nor did Montefiore believe that Jesus wished to found a new religion: "If he thought that the end was near, he can hardly have also intended to found a new religion and a new religious community."[8] Those aspects of Christian tradition that sharply remove Jesus from Judaism were, therefore, rejected by Montefiore.

In his view, the original Jesus belonged to the Liberal wing of Jewish tradition and should again be placed and accepted there. In part, Jesus can be regarded as belonging as much to Judaism as to Christianity.[9] Throughout his life Montefiore continued to honor him and to give him a very high place among the teachers of mankind. "I cannot conceive that a time will come when the figure of Jesus will no longer be a star of the first magnitude in the spiritual heavens, when he will no longer be regarded as one of the greatest religious heroes and teachers whom the world has seen."[10]

Jesus could be admired and understood within the framework of Judaism; it was much more difficult to deal with Paul. Montefiore tried to understand his life and his contribution to Christianity, attempting to see him within the framework of rabbinic Judaism. Contrary to many Jews he was not offended by the writings of Paul and sought to have Jews overlook Paul's historical inaccuracies. "In spite of his amazing forgetfulness of the Jewish doctrine of repentance and atonement, in spite, too, of the remoteness for us of his opposition 'Law versus Christ,' we may still admire the profundity of his genius and adopt many true and noble elements of his religious and ethical teaching. If we can exercise a careful eclecticism in Deuteronomy and Isaiah, we can also exercise it in the Epistle to the Romans and the Corinthians."[11] By doing this, however, Montefiore destroyed much of the "real" Paul and substituted a new individual.

Since Montefiore studied the New Testament and Christianity, we must be astonished by his neglect of previous Jewish writers in this area. He almost never quoted other Jews who had dealt with this subject, either to agree or disagree. Nor is his work particularly satisfying when viewed alongside the vast Christian scholarship of the late nineteenth century. Most of contemporary Christian scholarship was ignored. For example, he never dealt with Schweitzer's works on Jesus or Paul, although they had appeared early in the twentieth century. Montefiore was aware of German scholarship and reviewed German books in the *Jewish Quarterly Review*. His work was insular, as if the British Isles lay outside the world of scholarship. His books on Christianity did not win a wide audience. Christian scholars found them curiously outside the mainstream of study; Jews continued to view his efforts with suspicion, seeing him as too much an apologete for Christianity, especially Ahad Ha-am, who attacked him bitterly.[12]

Montefiore came closer to a dialogue with Christianity than any other thinker up to his time; many believe he went too far and thus began to surrender important elements of Judaism. He wrote about early Christian documents and heroes with warmth and affection, but he could do so only by ignoring the two millennia of later development. He felt justified in this selective approach because modern liberal Christianity appeared to be reemphasizing the key elements of early Christianity. By retaining the utopian spirit of the Victorian era well into the twentieth century, Montefiore seemed to be an anachronism. He looked forward to a universal religion, which would contain all that was noble and would transcend national boundaries. He longed for an end to whatever was old and narrow in both religions. His idealism blinded him to the horrors of our century. We must acknowledge the nobility of the effort, even while we recognize that his extremely liberal approach, which stripped so much away from both Judaism and Christianity, satisfied neither side.

The only individual in the first half of the century to engage in what appears to be dialogue was Franz Rosenzweig (1886–1929) who sought a new view of Christianity through his *Star of Redemption*. Christianity was no longer considered a secondary religion in its relationship to Judaism but a positive path to God. This work and his others were open to Christianity. They sought to strengthen modern Jewish faith by providing a different intellectual underpinning, but not at the expense of good relations with the surrounding world.

Franz Rosenzweig actually engaged in dialogue with Hans Ehrenberg through a series of letters. Although it has been tempting to view this as a real Christian-Jewish dialogue, it is nothing of the kind. After all Ehrenberg, his good friend, was a convert from Judaism who wondered why his friend Rosenzweig had not taken the same step. So we have a dialogue here between a Jew who has become ever more committed to Judaism and a former Jew who has followed a different religion. This dialogue, therefore, is really an in-house conversation.

Rosenzweig's approach to Christianity was influenced by his intense interest in Christianity during his youth. This led to a greater recognition of Christianity than most Jewish thinkers were willing to grant. On the other hand, his rejection of Christianity was vigorous and his critique, firm. Like Hermann Cohen before him, he was interested in the current philosophical overtones of Christianity. He felt that this was more important than an historical approach to events which had occurred some thousands of years before. The problems of the nineteenth century and the historicity of Jesus did not concern him. Furthermore, he felt no hesitation about dealing with the entire subject in a free and open manner. The fears of the previous century were gone. He was interested in building a new relationship with Christianity and made an attempt to do so without polemic.

As Rosenzweig understood Christianity in its relationship to Judaism, it had a special status granted to no other religion.[13] This did not mean that no truths had come from the pagan world, but paganism did not possess a system of truths. Paganism had no real approach to God, as had been granted to Judaism and through Judaism to Christianity. At best it could be classified as the pre-historic beginnings that led to the development of a higher form of religion.[14] In this way Rosenzweig ended any further discussion of pagan religions or pagan influence in the modern world. The whole problem was treated very differently by Max Brod (1884–1968), who felt that however one might classify the pagan elements in the modern world, they threatened to become predominant. In this matter, and in many other areas, Rosenzweig remained on a lofty philosophical plane without much consideration for realities. He still felt that Christianity was the way of the pagan to the God of Judaism. True as this might have been in the past, it did not reflect the conditions of the modern world. Rosenzweig never seriously considered the growing weakness of Christianity but continued to see it as a major force in twentieth century life.

Rosenzweig attempted to present the common basis of both religions symbolically with Israel as the "star" and Christianity the "rays"; this was central to his understanding of Christianity. "The truth, the entire truth, belongs neither to them nor to us. We bear it within ourselves, precisely, therefore, we must first gaze within ourselves, if we wish to see it. So we will see the star, but not its rays. To encompass the whole truth one must not only see the light but also what it illuminates. They, on the other hand, have been eternally destined to see the illuminated object, but not the light."[15] Truth, then, appears to man only in this divided form—the Jewish way and the Christian way—but before God it remains united. The unity exists, but only in the eyes of God; therefore, in our life and in the world there remain two truths.

Franz Rosenzweig cast a new light upon the relationship of Judaism and Christianity. He did not abandon the old distinctions and the historic differences, which had been discussed so often, but he tried to view them in a creative way. Some of his insights paralleled those of Buber and Baeck, whom he several times influenced directly. Rosenzweig built on the medieval Jewish thinkers; he did not reject their evaluation of Christianity but placed it in a different perspective. The ultimate distinctions and the final aim of Judaism remained the same; but because these elements had been transferred to the future, it was possible to achieve a much greater degree of understanding in the present.

Martin Buber (1878–1965) has touched many aspects of Jewish life and is undoubtedly the Jewish thinker most widely read among Christians in the western world. Buber studied Christianity for more than sixty years and wrote many essays on it. His approach was historical and philosophical. Jesus and Paul were the subject of special studies. He also engaged in one of the earliest Jewish-Christian dialogues—with the theologian Karl Ludwig Schmidt in 1933 in Stuttgart. The statements of both men were published; Buber subsequently expanded his presentation into a full book. Ironically, this forthright confrontation between the two religions occurred at the beginning of the Nazi period. In this dialogue Buber clearly presented his approach to Christianity: "We may attempt something very difficult, something very difficult for the man with religious ties; it strains his ties and relationships or rather seems to strain them. It seems to strain his relationship with God: We can acknowledge as a mystery that which someone else confesses as the reality of his faith, though it opposes our own existence and is contrary to the knowledge of our own being. We are not capable of judging its meaning, because we do not know it from within as we know ourselves from within."[16] Herewith Buber set the limits of his understanding of Christianity and any other religion, for it would be based only on external knowledge, which is deficient. Buber thus recognized the reality of Christianity as a path to God, as had Rosenzweig. This implies a demand for similar understanding and self-limitation by Christians who discuss Judaism.

Buber appreciated Jesus but rejected Paul. Like Montefiore and Baeck, he attempted to reclaim Jesus for Judaism, emphasizing the Jewish elements in his sayings. He considered Jesus a part of the Jewish tradition and wished to reclaim him for Judaism. He realized, however, that such reclamation was possible for Jesus but not for the later stages of Christianity.

Buber saw the need for a common emphasis on God and religion in the secularized twentieth century. "It behooves both you [Christians] and us [Jews] to hold inviolably fast to our own true faith, that is to our own deepest relationship to truth. It behooves both of us to show a religious respect for the true faith of the other. This is not what is called 'tolerance,' our task is not to tolerate each other's waywardness but to acknowledge the real relationship in which both stand to the truth. Whenever we both, Christian and Jew, care more for God himself than for our images of God, we are united in the feeling that our Father's house is differently constructed than our human models take it to be."[17] Both religions must continue along the paths set by their traditions, and they must leave the mystery of their simultaneous existence to God. Both will understand elements within each other's structures that are akin to their own, but they must learn not to condemn the rest. Buber hoped to interpret Christianity for Jews and to seek genuine dialogue with Christianity. Like Baeck, he did not allow the events of the twentieth century to destroy his hopes for better Judeo-Christian relations.

Major changes have occurred in the Judeo-Christian dialogue since the Second World War. The Holocaust, the establishment of the state of Israel in 1948, and the reorientation of Jewish life in the newly powerful United States along with changes in the Christian community have led to totally new paths for the Judeo-Christian dialogue. The shock of the Holocaust, especially after its magnitude had fully impressed itself on the Jewish community, led many to wonder whether an inter-religious dialogue was possible or desirable. Similar questions were raised by the Six Day War and Yom Kippur War when the existence of the state of Israel was threatened, yet even Christian leaders, who had participated in dialogue, remained largely silent or were suddenly inaccessible. This raised the question again and again whether we were actually engaging in serious conversation or whether this was an illusion.

Despite such doubts, a more optimistic view prevailed, and the effort continued with the chief impetus now coming from the American Jewish community. It found itself in the fortunate position of possessing a well established but not yet recognized intellectual basis which was constantly expanding. It was a successor to German Jewish learning, as the earlier German Jewish scholarship which combined Jewish knowledge with modernity had perished in the Holocaust. The self-assuredness of the American Jewish community paralleled that of America in the world. We felt secure in our international leadership and within our borders saw our rights steadily expand along with other ethnic groups. Along with the growing Jewish studies programs at public universities, it meant that a large number of individuals would be engaged. This response of the American Jewish community coincided with the establishment of the state of Israel and the feeling of pride in being co-founders and unswerving supporters of the new Jewish state. Its victories and vigor provided an additional basis for security. All of this brought a degree of frankness to the dialogue which had not existed earlier. Christians, stirred by the horror of the Holocaust, were willing to respond and new possibilities emerged.

A few Jewish thinkers provided the new impetus to dialogue after World War II. Among them was Samuel Sandmel (1911–1979) who dealt primarily with the first Christian century, its leading figures, and also with the biblical text on which much of their thought rests. He tried to place Jesus into a first century Jewish background although well aware of the difficulties which more careful study of the rabbinic text and the new discoveries at Qumram have demonstrated. His concept of Jesus, Paul, and others was open and much more objective and left room for further discussion.

Sandmel's books are intended as an introduction to Christianity for the Jew. In them he wished to break through the "vestigial sense of taboo." All of us, he said, are "in constant contact with this great body of religious expression that has become a cultural force in our secular environment."[18] Despite this desire he also points to the reasons for the Jewish disdain of Jesus and the New Testament. Long centuries of persecution made this field of study alien to most Jews; in addition, both Jews and Christians were kept apart by strong feelings of superiority.[19] Alongside his works for general readers, Sandmel has also produced many scholarly essays for the New Testament specialist.

Sandmel several times pointed to the danger in the uncritical use of rabbinic sources. He decried the feeling of superiority expressed by Strack and Billerbeck, who considered the statements of Jesus better than those of the rabbis, but he also pointed to the misuse of their work if the rabbinic and New Testament backgrounds of statements were not investigated. Some more recent Christian scholars feel this fault has been largely corrected; if this is so, then Samuel Sandmel could have felt that his efforts have met with success.

Sandmel dealt with all the books of the New Testament in a similarly sympathetic and scholarly manner. He was able to do so because "the New Testament, although it is not ours, is closer to us than any other sacred literature which is not our own." His work followed liberal Protestant scholarship, to which he has made special contributions.[20]

The contemporary scholar Samuel Tobias Lachs has made a contribution to the Judeo-Christian dialogue in the spirit of Sandmel through his *Rabbinic Commentary on the New Testament: The Gospels of Matthew, Mark and Luke.* In this book, Lachs sought to avoid Montefiore's bias toward Liberal Judaism and his limited emphasis on Jewish ethnicity as well as the problems of Strack and Billerbeck's *Kommentar Zum Neuen Testament*. Lach's work is straightforward and provides the reader, both Jewish and Christian, with a good introduction to some parallel sources for the gospels.

Hans Joachin Schoeps (1909–   ) resumed his involvement in the Judeo-Christian dialogue despite spending World War II as a refugee in Sweden. He was among the few Jewish scholars who returned to Germany quite early and who sought to reestablish a relationship between Germans and Jews. His books dealt primarily with first century Christianity and specifically with the very early Jewish Christians who had not yet broken away from Judaism. Like Benamozegh and Baeck before him, Schoeps understood Paul's view of the law as akin to the *halakhic* presumptions of other Jewish messianic groups like the Sabbatians. The law is valid only in our age and not in the eon after resurrection. Anyone who claims further validity for the law would reject Jesus as the messiah. However, Paul went farther and combined Jewish elements in an unusual pattern, which was original, but not acceptable to Judaism.

Schoeps' reconstruction of Ebionite theology and history met a sharp critical reception, yet his work also met a good deal of scholarly approval, and he had numerous Christian disciples.

Schoeps had some general thoughts on the relationship of the two religions. He felt that if progress was to occur, it would be necessary for both sides to acknowledge each other's truths, something they have not yet done. "Although we Jews will continue to reject the essence of Christian belief—that God, out of his infinite love for mankind, came down into flesh—we must change our attitude toward this event. . . . What is basically new—and at the same time also the utmost limit of what is possible—is this: We believe it when they say it. Therein lies the Jewish acknowledgement we have alluded to, namely to grant belief to the Christian witness that God has dealt with the world and a new revelation has taken place outside the covenant with Israel and the revelation to it." This will neither change nor abrogate Israel's special relationship to God. "The recognition of other covenants outside of Israel (sc. the covenant of Christ, and in principle, that of Mohammed) even fills a gap in Jewish knowledge, since according to Jewish belief, not only Israel, but all mankind belongs to God, and is called on the path to God."[21] Judaism cannot go farther than this, and it can only take this step if Christianity is willing to acknowledge the truth of Judaism in a similar manner. Following

Buber and others, Schoeps added that neither we nor they can understand each other's inner mystery.

In a totally different vein Richard Rubenstein (1924–   ) has provided a radical interpretation for both Jewish and Christian theology. In addition he has dealt with specific Christian figures and wrote a lengthy study of Paul. Rubenstein viewed Judaism and Christianity again in his *Religious Imagination,* in which he sought a psychoanalytic understanding of both religions.[22]

The solutions suggested by Rubenstein are novel but represent only an alternative for a post-Christian society. Similar conclusions are repeated in other essays in the same volume. Although Rubenstein can no longer believe in the myth of the chosen people, he sees no way in which "Jews can be entirely quit of this myth."[23] In his contribution to a symposium on Jewish belief, he does not find it necessary to claim a superior truth for Judaism over Christianity; yet he must "regard the claim of the Church vis-à-vis Judaism as inherently mistaken. . . . I find myself in the paradoxical position of asserting that Christianity is as true psychologically for Christians as Judaism is for Jews, while maintaining that the manifest claims of the Church concerning Israel and Israel's Messiah are without foundation."[24] Rubenstein has provided an entirely different basis for dialogue.

Emil Fackenheim (1915–   ) has been vigorous in his assault on the Christian basis for antisemitism and sought an approach to dialogue which was contemporary. Just before the Six Day War, when Fackenheim looked back upon the years of the Second World War and the problems of Israel, his attitude toward Christianity changed. "I am thus left with no doctrine, but only with openness to Jewish-Christian dialogue. But what is a religious recognition which does not recognize the other terms of his own self-understanding? The heart of dialogue, it seems to me, is to refuse to give an abstract answer to this question, and instead risk self-exposure. If Jew and Christian are both witnesses, they must speak from where they are. But unless they presume to be on the throne of divine judgment, they must listen as well as speak, risking self-exposure just because they are witnesses. For many years I believed that the long ago of Christian triumphalism over Judaism had ended and the age of Jewish-Christian dialogue had arrived. Today I am less sanguine."[25]

The Christian, according to Fackenheim, has been unwilling to understand Jewish survival and existence; he sees only a fossil, not a living religion. With some notable exceptions, Christians find it even more difficult to recognize Israel as a living state. These factors, as well as the inability of Christians to face up to their responsibility for the Holocaust, constitute the obstacles to a modern Judeo-Christian dialogue. Christians could not defend the state of Israel in 1967 because Christianity "failed to recognize the danger of the second Holocaust, for it still cannot face the fact of the first."[26]

Fackenheim entirely avoided the usual categories of discussion. He felt strongly that secularism threatens both Judaism and Christianity with destruction, even as German-Christian antisemitism brought the Holocaust. Judeo-Christian understanding will only come if we unite to face secularism. This necessity makes all other discussions superfluous. Both Judaism and Christianity must expose themselves to the secular world, for that is "where the action is." We must struggle against it together. This is a bond uniting both religions, although we have only recently begun to understand this.[27]

Two European scholars who have reemphasized an approach to dialogue through historical studies should be noted. Shalom Ben-Chorin, who lives in Israel but writes in German for Germans, has written on Jesus, Paul, and Mary in a way which combines history and theology. His more popular approach has proven influential in Germany. He is the only Jewish thinker who has dealt with Mary. His reconstruction of her life and influence is not without problems. The positive approach of this Israeli has helped the German dialogue.[28]

Geza Vermes (1924–   ), the English historian, has continued to feel that without an understanding of first century events there can be no real basis for dialogue. His historical views of early Christianity have developed through a masterful reworking of Emil Schuerer, *The History of the Jewish People in the Age of Jesus Christ.* In two books published a decade apart,[29] Vermes has set out to provide a thorough account of the life and times of Jesus within the Jewish setting. In both these works Vermes seeks an objective approach which avoids the apologetics and polemics of both Jewish and Christian historians. He sees the historical Jesus in the complex setting of first century Judaism as well as the Greco-Roman world and seeks to explain the tensions of the time, the reactions of various Jewish groups, as well as the nature of Jesus' own harsh comments through this setting. This series of studies has dealt with only one aspect of the life and understanding of Jesus, and Vermes has promised that others will follow. Geza Vermes has placed Jesus into an historical framework which is sound and provides a starting point for historical discussions.

David Novak (1941–   ) is among the few traditional Jewish thinkers willing to engage in dialogue. Most traditional Jews consider authentic dialogue between the two religions neither possible nor desirable.

David Novak made a distinction between dialogue which engages a secular Jew and a secular Christian for whom the main differences between the two religions have been removed through emphasis on the secular morality, and dialogue between believers. He considers dialogue important as all believers Jewish and Christian are endangered by the onslaught of the secular world.

Novak approached through the great *halakhists* and philosophers of the past. He traced Jewish attitudes to paganism and Christianity from the Noahide laws through medieval *halakhists* like Rabenu Tam and Menahem Ha-Meiri, and indicated the basis on which these Jewish scholars were able to view Christians as fellow monotheists, and no longer as pagans. He then discussed in considerable detail Maimonides' developing view of Christianity.[30]

As the historical segment of the book comes closer to the present day, Novak discussed the various Reform Jewish approaches, particularly on the American scene in the late nineteenth century. According to Novak, the optimism of the times led both the Jewish and Christian participants astray. Furthermore, the effort to find a new basis for Judaism, made by individuals like Mendelssohn, and, much later, Kauffman Kohler, was not a proper foundation for Novak's interpretation of Judaism. Novak criticized both Baeck and Buber for their apologetic approach.

Novak concluded that although there is a Judeo-Christian ethic, there is no Judeo-Christian faith. The common Hebrew Bible and the belief in its "authentic revelation" provide a foundation shared by Judaism and Christianity. He listed four theological affirmations which he felt were the ground on which the dialogue could be built.

1. The human person is created by God for the primary purpose of being related to God.

2. This relationship with God is primarily practical, its content being response to commandment from God.

3. The human person is created as a social being. This sociality is the human pre-condition for covenant with God; that is, singular divine revelation is to an historically extant community of persons, not to isolated individuals. Human response to such singular revelation is, then, within the context of such a covenantal community. Thus the covenant presupposes a general morality of socially pertinent standards as well as entailing specific intercovenantal norms.

4. The ultimate fulfillment of human personhood, both individually and collectively, lies in a future and universal redemptive act by God, one as yet on the unattainable historical horizon. He stated that these are the affirmations which separate both Judaism and Christianity from the other moral options which are available to modern individuals and can be subsumed under the headings of autonomy and heteronomy. Both Jews and Christians find themselves as opponents to the modern secular world. Each must reflect his authentic position and see the other in a recognizable manner. Jews need not give up their understanding of the divine election of Israel and the revelation of the Torah, nor need Christians give up their belief in Jesus and his special status. Neither party needs to engage in apologetics or lose itself in historical debate."[31]

Novak's approach differed from those who preceded him, as he placed no emphasis on first century events. Instead he dealt with the theological distinctions between the two faiths. He also showed little concern with recent history, the Holocaust or Israel. As both religious and secular Jews have been, and continue to be, influenced by these events, this represents a shortcoming in Novak's approach. He is keenly aware of the powerful secular world with which both religions must contend, and seeks to enhance the possibilities of dialogue in order to strengthen both faiths in their struggle with the secular world.

Eugene Borowitz (1924–   ), the leading theologian of Liberal Judaism, has provided a totally different approach to Christianity. Instead of concentrating on the first century or the historical figures of the past he has dealt exclusively with the current world in his *Contemporary Christologies: A Jewish Response* (1980). His treatment of christologies is unique; no other Jewish thinker has treated this aspect of Christianity. His approach is different not only in this way, but as it combines theology with a more personal tone it is not as stiff as Leo Baeck or Franz Rosenzweig.

Borowitz has engaged in conversation with many of the individuals he discusses. He is fully aware of the different cross-currents in the Christian intellectual world and has reacted from his own Liberal Jewish stance. One may very well say that Eugene Borowitz and David Novak have each approached modern Christianity from their particular understanding of Judaism. Although Novak would deny the validity of the Liberal stance, Borowitz clearly demonstrates its vigor and the positive manner through which it is capable of dealing with Christianity. The world of Christian theology is far removed from the concern of most Jewish scholars and so appears only peripherally in their thinking; however, it is primary for Christianity. For this reason this work is an important addition to the dialogue.

As we look back over the last quarter of a century as well as previous efforts, we can see franker dialogue developing. The safely worded statements of an earlier period have been replaced by forthright historical descriptions and challenges. A large number of Jewish and Christian writers have dealt with the anti-Jewish bias and the outright antisemitism expressed in various Christian documents beginning with the New Testament and continuing on through the medieval, renaissance and modern period. Furthermore, scholarship no longer concentrates entirely on an understanding of Jesus, Paul, and the New Testament but has expanded to include modern Christian theology. A large number of other Jewish scholars who cannot be mentioned here have written monographs and essays in this field. They and the institutions, presses and journals which have encouraged them deserve recognition, but the space of this paper does not permit it.

All this has meant that it is now possible to approach the theme of Jewish Christian relationship from more new perspectives than at an earlier time. We can therefore say that the Judeo-Christian dialogue, which in its scholarly guise had only a handful of participants before the Second World War, has now emerged as a field of academic as well as popular religious endeavor. *Nostra Aetate* has helped the process.

NOTES

1. Leo Baeck, "Some Questions to the Christian Church from the Jewish Point of View," in *The Church and the Jewish People,* ed. Gote Hedenquist (London, 1954), pp. 102f.

2. "Romantic Religion," in Leo Baeck, *Judaism and Christianity,* trans. Walter Kaufmann (Philadelphia, 1958), p. 290.

3. R. Mayer, *Christentum und Judentum,* pp. 52ff.

4. Ibid. p. 57.

5. Leo Baeck, "Some Questions to the Christian Church from the Jewish Point of View," p. 116.

6. Claude G. Montefiore, *Outlines of Liberal Judaism* (London, 1923), p. 316.

7. Idem, *The Synoptic Gospels* (London, 1927), p. xxiv.

8. Ibid. p. cxxxvi.

9. Claude G. Montefiore, *Some Elements of the Religious Teaching of Jesus According to the Synoptic Gospels* (London, 1910), p. 9; *Outlines of Liberal Judaism,* pp. 330f.

10. *Outlines of Liberal Judaism,* p. 336.

11. Montefiore, *Liberal Judaism* (London 1903), p. 174.

12. Ahad Ha-am, "Al sh'teh ha-s'ifim," *Al Parashat Derakim* (Berlin, 1925), vol. 4, pp. 38ff.

13. Franz Rosenzweig, *Der Stern der Erlösung* (Heidelberg, 1930), 2:39f, 100f, 179ff.

14. "Das neue Denken," in Franz Rosenzweig, *Kleinere Schriften* (Berlin, 1937), p. 382; also *Briefe,* pp. 512f.

15. *Der Stern der Erlösung,* 3:200ff.

16. Martin Buber, *Die Stunde und die Erkenntnis* (Berlin, 1936), p. 152.

17. Martin Buber, *Israel and the World* (New York, 1948), p. 40.

18. Samuel Sandmel, *Jewish Understanding of the New Testament* (Cincinnati, 1956), p. xi.

19. Idem, *We Jews and Jesus* (New York, 1965), pp. 7ff.

20. See Bibliography, in idem, *The First Christian Century,* pp. 231–32.

21. Hans-Joachim Schoeps, *The Jewish Christian Argument* (New York, 1963), pp. 165ff.

22. Richard Rubenstein, *The Religious Imagination* (New York, 1968), p. 165.

23. Idem, "Symposium on Jewish Belief," *After Auschwitz* (New York, 1966), p. 147.

24. Ibid. p. 149.

25. "These Twenty Years," in Emil Fackenheim, *Quest for Past and Future* (London, 1968), p. 22.

26. Ibid. p. 25.

27. "On Self-Exposure of Faith to the Modern Secular World," ibid. p. 285.

28. Shalom Ben-Chorin, *Bruder Jesus. Der Nazarener in jüdischer Sicht* (Munich, 1967); *Paulus. Der Völkerapostel in jüdischer Sicht* (Munich, 1970); *Mutter Mirjam. Maria in jüdischer Sicht* (Munich, 1971).

29. Geza Vermes, *Jesus the Jew,* (Philadelphia, 1973); *Jesus and the World of Judaism* (Philadelphia, 1983).

30. David Novak, *The Image of the Non-Jew in Judaism* (Montreal, 1983); *Jewish-Christian Dialogue, a Jewish Justification* (Oxford, 1989).

31. Idem, *The Jewish-Christian Dialogue,* p. 141.

A Jewish Theological Understanding
of Christianity in Our Time

David Novak

1. THE COMPLEXITY OF THE
JEWISH-CHRISTIAN RELATIONSHIP

My late revered teacher, Professor Abraham Joshua Heschel, was the first major Jewish theologian in America to enter into dialogue with Christian theologians on a high theological level, in the early 1960s. Once, at that time, when I was part of a small group of students who regularly met with him in a seminar in Jewish theology, he openly wondered, and invited us to wonder with him, what the history of Judaism would have been if the vast majority of the Jewish people had begun to move eastward to Asia rather than westward to Europe after the destruction of the second temple in the first century of the Common Era.

What would have become of Judaism if the center of Jewry had taken root in India or China, for example, rather than in Spain and the Rhineland. What would have become of Judaism in civilizations whose character was formulated by religions such as Hinduism or Buddhism, which themselves had no original connection with Judaism at all? By implication, the question is, also, what would have become of Judaism if the historical connection with Christianity had ceased shortly after the birth of the new Christian religion, if the connection with Judaism and the Jewish people had not persisted, and the mother religion and daughter religion had soon ceased to live in any kind of real proximity and share any continuing history. Would Judaism and the Jewish people have fared better or worse if they had not found themselves for the most part living in a civilization dominated by the Christian religion, which has claimed all along to be the direct descendant and fulfillment of Judaism and the life of the Jewish people. (The same question, *mutatis mutandis,* could be asked about Jewish involvement with Islam, a religion that also claims, although to a much lesser extent than Christianity, descent from Judaism.)

Since my teacher raised this question to us at the very time he was engaged in intense dialogue with the leaders of the Roman Catholic Church as they were preparing for Vatican Council II, I did not take his question to us, either then or now, to be one of idle historical speculation. Rather, I have always taken it to be his warning that only the most rigorous theological approach will be equal to the challenge of understanding what has, no doubt, been the most complex interreligious relationship in human history. "According to the effort, so is the reward," the ancient rabbis taught.[1] In my own theological wrestling as a Jew with Judaism's relationship with Christianity, I have tried not to forget his warning. To me it has always said: Be cautious but hopeful.[2]

Because Judaism and Christianity have been in such constant historical contact, theological analysis of that relationship must begin to research its complex past. Yet the present situation and its future projections must first be constituted if the past is to be included in a theological reflection, but not subsume it. Theological reflection takes place within history, but the history within which it takes place is an ongoing, open-ended, process. The present and its future extensions must call upon the past for resources without ever assuming, however, that the answers sought are already there intact.[3]

In this particular theological reflection I intend to first concentrate on what the relationship between Judaism and Christianity *was* for much of the past, *pre-modern* period of the parallel history of the two communities. Next I intend to concentrate on what the relationship *has been* for much of the present or *modern* period. Finally, I intend to concentrate on what I think the relationship *is to be* in at least the immediate future visible on the historical horizon, in what has already been called by many the *post-modern* world. This final concentration is not an act of futuristic speculation of what *might be.* Rather, it is an act of moral judgment. It is the responsibility I consider Jews and Christians now have if they are committed to the continuing deepening and improvement of their mutual relationship from the present and beyond, a deepening and improvement which has already been made manifest of late to some Jews and some Christians in history.

2. THE LEGACY OF DISPUTATIONISM

Actual theological contacts between Jews and Christians during much of the pre-modern period are best characterized as disputations. Even when not engaging in literal face-to-face disputations, Jews and Christians were speaking about each other in essentially disputational terms. Disputational thinking was conducted in two forms: one that might be called rejectionist, the other accommodationist.

In rejectionist type disputation, each religion regarded the other as something to be totally delegitimized.

For Christians, as is well known, this meant that the Jews were in fact impostors, people still claiming to be the elect nation of God, Israel, when in truth the church had totally superseded the Jews in that role with God.[4] The very existence of the Jewish people as a religious community separate from Christianity was regarded as a fundamental affront to the new religious community with whom God had now made his permanent covenant. The legitimacy of the Jews *qua* Jews was something that belonged to history as the past, rather than to history as the ongoing life of the present into the future.

The affront was that those who were supposed to have belonged only to the past were insisting on being present and extending themselves into the future, without at all affirming the Christian view of the present (*kairos*) and future (*parousia*). The social, economic, political and legal ramifications of this rejectionist view of Jews and Judaism were enormous, considering that so much of pre-modern western civilization was indeed *Christendom,* where Christians held political power and justified their power in Christian terms.

Because Jews did not have actual political power over Christians, Jewish rejectionism as regards Christianity was unable to express itself within the real dynamics of history. Nevertheless, this view certainly existed (and still exists in some Jewish circles) and it influenced Jewish attitudes toward Christians and Christianity all along. The sources upon which this Jewish rejectionism drew are important to examine because, fortunately, they admit of more than one interpretation and more than one application.

· It can be well demonstrated that, as far as biblical teaching goes, idolatry is only proscribed for Jews. Nowhere in the Hebrew Bible is there any explicit prohibition of idolatry for Gentiles. This distinction seems to be based on the fact that idolatry is a sin only subsequent to Israel's becoming covenanted with God. The essence of the biblical prohibition of idolatry is "You shall have no other gods in my presence" (Ex 20:3). In biblical teaching, God's omnipresence is not something inferred from the experience of nature. Rather, it is declared by revelation. Once God has appeared to his people and covenanted with them, no other god is *thereafter* acceptable *for them.*

That is why idolatry is so often compared to adultery. In adultery there can only be a sin after one of the adulterers is already married to someone else. So it is with idolatry (in this view anyway)—there is only a sin after Israel is in the covenant. Those outside the covenant lack the very pre-condition for culpability for the sin of idolatry. Only Israel can be guilty of it. And although the Bible recognizes the existence of individual non-Jewish monotheists, they are regarded in one way or another as "invisible" extensions of the covenanted people of Israel. Nevertheless, on the level of peoples, monotheistic Israel (at least in principle) was on one side and all the polytheistic Gentile nations were on the other. "Our God is in heaven, doing whatever he wants; but their idols are silver and gold, the works of human hands" (Ps 115:3–4). The idea of a monotheistic community of Gentiles was simply inconceivable.

In the rabbinic period, this neat division between Jews and Gentiles was radically changed. During that period there emerged the rabbinic doctrine of the seven Noahide laws, which are seven categories of commandments considered binding on all humankind (who are the descendants of Noah after the flood). While there were various disputes among the rabbis themselves about what these laws actually are, and even whether they are more or less than seven in number, in every version of them the prohibition of idolatry for Gentiles is found in a prominent place, if not the most prominent place. What we have here, then, is that the proscription of idolatry is no longer a corollary of the covenant with Israel. Rather, it both antedates it (the Noahide laws predate the Sinaitic laws) and it reaches beyond it (humankind extends farther than the boundaries of Israel). This doctrine radically changed the way Jews looked at the non-Jewish world. Whereas in the biblical view the non-Jewish world was regarded as one idolatrous monolith, varying only in terms of the moral quality of interhuman practices, in the rabbinic view the non-Jewish world was now rent in two: one part idolatrous, the other monotheistic.

The doctrine of Noahide law, and most importantly the doctrine of the universal prohibition of idolatry, gave Jewish thinkers the criterion they needed to judge the two religions among whose adherents they had to live from late antiquity on: Christianity and Islam. Generally Islam, because of its strict monotheism and absolute prohibition of the use of images, received a more positive judgment from Jewish thinkers than did Christianity with its trinitarianism and liturgical use of images. Because of this, in a number of areas of Jewish law which govern contacts between Jews and non-Jews, Muslims were judged more favorably than Christians.[5]

At this level, then, the Jewish rejection of Christianity was every bit as harsh as the Christian rejection of Judaism. Whether this harsh Jewish judgment of Christianity would have translated into the same type of social, political, economic and legal restrictions, if Jews had the same type of power over Christians that Christians did have over them, is like all historical speculation—unanswerable. Truth to tell, one cannot say it would have been impossible.

I mention this to assuage the tendency of some well-meaning Christians, who are sincerely committed to improving the Christian relationship with Judaism, to assume that all malevolent obstacles to that improvement come from the Christian side, and that the Jewish side contains only benevolence. Christian malevolence, to be sure, had more of an opportunity to apply itself in history than did Jewish malevolence. However, hard theological rethinking of traditional options is required from both sides. In terms of the dialogue as a human activity, its purposes are much better served by two active partners than by one active (and guilt-ridden) partner and the other passive (and self-righteous).[6]

Fortunately, for those now committed to the improvement of the Jewish-Christian relationship, the rejectionist interpretation of the classical Jewish sources, as they apply to Christianity, is not the only option. In the later middle ages there emerged a more positive view of Christianity, one which could be termed accommodationist.[7] In this view, Christianity is not judged to be idolatrous. The reasons for this new judgment were basically two: one strictly theological, the other more juridical.

On the theological level, it was now assumed that even despite Christian worship of the Trinity, the ultimate object of Christian worship and allegiance is the God who is creator of heaven and earth. In other words, Christians and Jews are really bound to the same God, albeit in different ways. The difference between Judaism and Christianity, which in the rejectionist view is a difference in kind, in the accommodationist view is one of degree. In this view the difference between Jews and Christians is that Jews *in* the covenant have a direct, unmediated relationship with God, whereas Christians *through* Jesus have an indirect, mediated relationship with this same God. Moreover, the northern European thinkers who advocated this view (unlike their contemporary Jewish thinkers in Spain) were in no wise adherents of Aristotelian philosophy and its natural theology, which argued that God's existence could be demonstrated outside of historical revelation. As such, it can only be assumed that they gave this theological approval of Christianity because Christianity accepted the creator God as he has revealed himself in the Hebrew Bible.

On the juridical level, it was now recognized by many Jewish thinkers that Christianity had explicitly accepted the moral teaching of the Hebrew Bible as normative. And, unlike Islam, it accepted that source of its moral teaching precisely because it is God's revelation to his people Israel, and it is as Israel has preserved it in scripture. Thus, Christianity was now regarded by many (but by no means all) Jewish thinkers as a lesser version of Judaism, for Gentiles.

This type of accommodationist theology is still very much part of the thinking of most traditional Jews who have a generally positive view of Christianity as a Gentile religion. Indeed, the basic logic of this position has easily recognizable analogues in Christian thinking about Jews, thinking which has a generally positive view of Judaism. It is the notion that the body of Israel or the body of the church extends, in a descending sense to be sure, beyond the range of its literal adherents.

Despite the attractiveness of this accommodationist approach, certainly when contrasted with the rejectionist approach that, we have seen, is found in both Jewish and Christian tradition, it is still inadequate on both historical and philosophical grounds.[8]

On historical grounds it is inadequate because it takes what is essentially a late medieval view and catapults it into contemporary discussion, in effect ignoring the whole onslaught of modernity. Modernity must be first understood and then overcome if the Jewish-Christian relationship is to locate itself in the real historical situation before us now. It cannot simply be detoured.

On philosophical grounds it is inadequate for purposes of dialogue, which this relationship should optimally be, because its portrayal of the other faith (be it by Jews of Christianity, or by Christians of Judaism) is one which the other faith—in good faith—cannot possibly accept about itself. There is no true dialogue when each side is relating to a phantom of its own projection, however benevolent that projection might be, rather than to a view of the dialogue partner that the other can truly accept.

Christians cannot be faithful to their covenantal commitment, with true cogency, by regarding themselves as essentially Jewish derivatives.[9] And Jews cannot remain faithful to their covenantal commitment, with true cogency, by regarding themselves as essentially proto-Christians. This approach, then, only allows each religious community to view the other from afar, with a certain amount of genuine respect. But that view is one which is only theological, taking theology in the strictest sense, namely, without the incorporation of philosophical and historical perspectives. It is theological in this strict sense because it is cogent in those areas where there is no real interrelationship between Jews and Christians and where there neither can nor should be one.

At this interior level, what might be termed the sacramental life of each respective community, each community must regard its own truth as superior to all others. At best, these other truths can be regarded as only derivative in some way or other. Although this interior level is where the heart of each religious community must be recognized and guarded, it is not wholly sufficient for the full life of that community in the world. Before the enlightenment that was less apparent (although still true) than it has been since then. Religious communities before the enlightenment could live in far greater isolation than they do now. A growing interaction between religious communities has been brought about by the fact that the world in which all of them live is far greater than any of them combined. As such, they are called upon to engage in reflection which, in order to be theologically informed continually, must extend beyond theology proper into the areas of philosophy and history.

3. THE MODERN ALTERNATIVE

The coming of the enlightenment in the eighteenth century, with its subsequent political emancipation of the Jews in western Europe, radically changed the context of all social and cultural relationships. The relationship between Jews and Christians can be seen as a prime example of that change.

Up until that time, the relationship between Jews and Christians, viewed from either side, was one whose ultimate meaning could only be located within the overall covenantal relationship between God and his people. That relationship always had absolute primacy. It was the one that basically determined all interhuman relationships, first within the covenanted community itself and then between the covenanted community and the outside world.

With the enlightenment, all that changed within western European (and, by extension, American) culture. Whereas, before, God had been the measure of all things, man now occupied that central role. Although this anthropocentric emphasis can be seen (a point that contemporary rationalists would dispute, however) as eventually leading to an acceptance of unrestrained human will, in the enlightenment the emphasis was on the primacy of man as a rationally autonomous ethical being, fully capable of constructing a meaningful world for himself. Every human being is to be considered as an end-in-itself, as Kant most famously put it.[10] The structure of all human relationships is to be philosophically worked up from that intuition as its practical application.

Theology now had to justify itself ethically, by various forms of philosophical argument. The relationship between God and man, with which theology (Jewish and Christian) is primarily concerned, could only be postulated if it contributed to rounding out the cogency of ethical theory. Moreover, the only divine-human relationship that this new anthropocentrism would tolerate was between a postulated deity and the human individual. As for the more historically precedented covenantal relationships between God and peoples, the only role left for them—and the patterns of ritualized culture they had produced—was that there be selected those practices that could be justified as contributing to the overall functioning of the ethically autonomous individual.

The primacy of theology, either as it had affected the complexities of the Protestant-Catholic relationship, or the complexities of the Christian-Jewish relationship, was seen as something that needed to be bracketed, if not eventually limited altogether. Concerning our specific topic in this essay, it could be said that acceptance of the enlightenment was seen as enabling Jews and Christians to relate to one another primarily as a-historical individuals, and that the particular historical baggage they still carried with them as members of covenanted communities was relegated to the background.

Secularism had now proclaimed what seemed to many Christians, and even many more Jews (proportionally), to be a simple solution to what had theretofore been a complex situation, one entailing much intolerance and suffering. Thus, understanding the lure of secularism for many

modern Jews, the late Jesuit theologian and political theorist John Courtney Murray once wrote:

> There is the ancient resentment of the Jew, who has for centuries been
> dependent for his existence on the good will, often not forthcoming, of a
> Christian community. Now in America, where he has acquired social
> power, his distrust of the Christian community leads him to align him-
> self with the secularizing forces whose dominance, he thinks, will afford
> him a security he has never known.[11]

4. THE INADEQUACY OF THE MODERN ALTERNATIVE

The inadequacy of the modern, secularist, alternative to medieval
disputationism (whether of the rejectionist or accommodationist type) is
to assume that humans can transcend their traditions and simply recon-
stitute themselves in an a-historical realm, one whose simplicity and transparent rationality greatly overcome the confusing complexities of the
past. That is the enlightenment project, which certainly still has many
adherents even today.

It is now being argued, however, especially by the contemporary philosopher Alasdair MacIntyre, that the enlightenment is a failure by its
own criterion of the transcendence of historical limitations. MacIntrye
and others have shown that the enlightenment itself is as much a product
of its own particular culture as that which it proclaimed to have success-
fully overcome.[12]

If all thinking, then, is conducted within the context of a cultural
tradition, it seems to be more consistent and fruitful to be explicit about
contextual limitations, and not pretending to be what it is not and cannot
be. This historical contextualization has even been shown to be highly
plausible about the thinking of the natural sciences, especially by the
historian of science, Thomas Kuhn.[13] I mention this because the propo-
nents of the enlightenment always pointed to the great success of the
natural sciences in the modern world as being due to their transcendence
of cultural limitations. Thus, if such transcendence of history does not
even apply to the natural sciences anymore, how much less does it apply
to thinking about the relationship between Judaism and Christianity,
where historical considerations must always be kept explicit.

In terms of this relationship in our own, post-modern world, it means
that Jews and Christians can only develop an authentic relationship when

they attempt to discover where their respective traditions overlap and when they discover what is the common border that they share in the world. The relationship is inauthetic, however, when some sort of new, neutral position is posited, where both sides are to transcend traditions whose limitations are now to be resented.

At this stage of history, Jews should realize that the enlightenment took much more from them than it gave. It basically asked Jews to divest themselves of everything that made them unique, and to become part of a new social order where the same divestment was supposed to be done by everyone else as well. The fact was, however, that these "others," namely, the Christian majority, were not required to do anything so radical. They were merely asked to transform their tradition into something more rational and more anthropocentric. Nevertheless, virtually all of the traditional Christian symbols were left intact, however much they were recontextualized.

From the fact of this unequal demand, it was clear that Jewish-Christian mutuality was essentially illusionary in this context. When it existed, it was largely an issue for Jews, who had already divested themselves of just about everything that made them singularly Jewish, *hoping* that Christians would soon do the same. But when these secularized Jews became impatient with what they took to be Christian recalcitrance in this secularizing process, and when they demanded it be speeded up, many Christians became quite resentful. Jews were seen as the enemies of Christian tradition, indeed of all tradition. This negative impression has not been helped by the fact that, for the most part, those Jews who have been most conspicuous in the politics of secular society have been the least Jewish in terms of their religious commitment.[14] The vast majority of the most religiously committed Jews, on the other hand, have tried to remain as inconspicuous as possible in this context, carefully guarding their ethnic isolation, which the secularized and secularizing society has been willing, so far, to overlook as quaint ethnic enclaves.

5. THE POST-MODERN OPPORTUNITY
FOR JEWS AND CHRISTIANS

In our age, when the pretensions of the enlightenment are becoming more and more apparent, Jews and Christians who still believe that their respective religious traditions can speak to them, and to the world beyond them as well, now have an important opportunity to speak to each other in a new way. If thoughtful members of both communities are adequately aware of the moment they now occupy in history, and are prepared to re-search their respective traditions for the resources there to be developed for this moment, then the Jewish-Christian relationship has a good chance of becoming something more enriching than it has ever been heretofore. Here is where the theological challenge lies, understanding "theology" in its wider rather than its stricter sense.

The pretensions of the enlightenment have been nowhere more apparent than in the very area where it claimed to have staked out new, fundamental ground: ethics. The notion of the human individual as a rational, self-legislating being has been challenged as an actual affront to both the human connection with history and the human connection with nature. Both connections are violated when the essence of humanness is posited as *homo faber.*

On the historical level, it has been shown that ethics primarily functions as the norm for humans-in-community. The voluntary associations of human beings characterized by contractual arrangements (hence the "social contract" so persistently advocated by enlightenment thinkers from John Locke in the seventeenth century to John Rawls in the twentieth) are clearly subsequent to and dependent on the older ways in which humans are related to one another through communal bonds. These bonds are prior to human invention and stipulation. For this reason, much of traditional ethics has been concerned with familial relationships. This reality, in particular, is one to which the enlightenment is simply unprepared to address itself because it is neither within the domain of the individual at the one end or the state at the other. These are the only two domains which the enlightenment can recognize and constitute.

In our age, when there is so much confusion over issues of sexual ethics—all of which are family issues in one way or another—the enlightenment and its adherents have little to say. In their view of the world, all ethical issues become questions of civil liberties, which is increasingly being shown to be a far too simplistic model to guide society in dealing with such complex moral problems as incest, abortion, divorce and substance abuse.[15]

Although new challenges in this area call for fresh thinking on the part of all members of our society, Jews and Christians are better prepared to deal with them inasmuch as they have not severed their links with tradition. Since the family is the prime unit in the transmission of tradition (indeed, tradition itself has little meaning for those uprooted from family), it stands to reason that the grave familial problems our society faces at present can only be cogently approached within the context of tradition.

On the level of nature, it is becoming more and more evident that the pretensions of *homo faber* as the essential definition of humanness are the prime cause of the worsening ecological crisis we face. We are suffering more and more from our technological programs based on the assumption that the earth (and the sky) is an infinite resource at our disposal, something which belongs to us and is to be used for whatever project we happen to be creating in our own image. It is not just that we need a more intelligent technology, one which will be more sensitive to the long-range effects of our own projects than has been the case heretofore. Rather, technology itself is now the issue in the sense that we are being required to rethink our mutual relationship with our fellow inhabitants of the earth, both human and non-human, and with what lies beyond the surface of this planet. This latter point is most immediately impressed upon us of late by issues pertaining to the atmosphere and extraterrestrial projection.

Here again, without the fundamentalist claim to have a ready-made answer for every question in advance, Jews and Christians are in a better position to face those grave issues in relation to nature because they have been nurtured by the doctrine of creation. The doctrine of creation has taught us that we humans are not the works of our own hands—"He made us and not we ourselves" (Ps 100:3)[16]—and that the earth itself "is given to humankind" (Ps 115:16), not for its own disposal, but only "to work for it and care for it" (Gen 2:15). The exalted place of man and woman in the order of creation, precisely because it is not of their own making but a ministry to which they are appointed, is what makes the commandment to be responsible for the rest of earthly creation intelligible.

Thus, Jews and Christians, both informed by what they have learned about the integrity of creation from the Hebrew Bible, need not try to invent ecological ethics *de novo*. Indeed, that project itself is trapped in a paradox: How does one *invent* a criterion for containing *invention?* (*Quis custodiet ipsos custodios?*) Rather, Jews and Christians have a resource for developing approaches that both respect the integrity of creation and the integrity of the unique human creature therein, one who is in some ways part of it, and in some ways is not.

6. JEWISH-CHRISTIAN COOPERATION IN THE POST-MODERN AGE

The question, then, is: How can Jews and Christians bring these considerable resources to the world at large?

The first point that emerges from the acceptance of this challenge is that neither Jews nor Christians can do it alone, in our society at least. For in our society today, the usual secularist reaction in dealing with the message brought to society by any particular community is to automatically assume that the message is from a "special interest group," one whose motives are those of self-interest, even when hidden behind a seemingly altruistic rhetoric. In this view, the task of secular society is to balance the message of one community against those of other communities and to try to find some consensus among all of them. If the secularists involved are still old-fashioned enlightenment rationalists, this consensus will be one in which the rights of the individual remain the ultimate criterion for judging the often conflicting claims of various, particular communities.

Jews and Christians in our society have all too easily fallen into this secularist trap and been naively willing to present their message to the world under the rubric of special interest. The reasoning behind this adjustment is that it is the only way to survive in a secular world. Nevertheless, by so doing, these Jews and Christians have lost sight of who they are and what their message to the world really is. For the true claims of Jews and Christians are based on the doctrine of revelation, which means that they are essentially the recipients of a message about the world, one which is given to them from the only source who can see the world from the perspective of real transcendence—*sub specie divinitatis.* They claim to be the recipients of the word of God, the God who created the world and who promises to redeem it.

When, however, this message is proclaimed by only one community, simultaneously making exclusivistic and triumphalistic claims about itself, claims which more often than not delegitimize all others, the public credibility of the message becomes highly suspect. For the claims of the community on its own behalf are frequently more emphatic than the message proclaimed to and for the world. As such, it appears to be another case of special pleading by one more special interest group in society. By setting itself up to be so categorized and characterized, any religious community eclipses the very intent of its message altogether.

When, on the other hand, Jews and Christians discover their common border that faces onto the world, and devise means for the joint proclamation of certain truths they hold in common, the public credibility of their message increases enormously. It increases because the animosity which, truly but unfortunately, characterized so much of the relationship between the two communities throughout history is now being overcome by these two communities themselves. The secularist assumption, conversely, has been that the only way to overcome interreligious animosity is to essentially remove "religion"—in reality, that means removing Judaism and Christianity—from public influence altogether.[17]

The religious communities themselves, however, are beginning to accomplish for themselves and for the world what secularism could not do because it demanded what is culturally impossible. When Jews and Christians now have something in common to say jointly to the world, and that message is not one which simply promotes some issue immediately benefiting both communities politically, many of the secularist stereotypes about the necessarily religious character of public animosity are then belied. It is a good deal more difficult to continue reducing the message to a case of special pleading under these new historical circumstances. Moreover, it stands to reason that if something is true for the world at large, that truth should surely have been discovered by more than one community alone.

This joint proclamation of certain truths about the nature of the human person and human community as created historical realities cannot be made, however, in a didactic way. It cannot be done in a way which basically says to the world: We already have the truth, and you must now accept it from us! That method of relating to the moral issues of the world cannot be applied for two reasons.

First, Judaism and Christianity do not operate from the same basis of authority. In both communities, it is not the unmediated voice from scripture which is sufficiently normative, but rather the voice of scripture as interpreted by the traditional community and its structure of authority. Here, at this level, Judaism and Christianity cannot speak with the same voice; both cannot and dare not jointly proclaim "Thus saith the Lord." The word of God for Judaism and Christianity, respectively, is materially inseparable from the communal medium who proclaims it. Christians cannot in good faith look to Jewish authorities for the normative meaning of the word of God any more than Jews in good faith can look to Christian authorities for it. The only way this could be done, without total surrender of one religious community to the other, would be some sort of syncretism between the two communities. But the respective traditions of both communities have carefully proscribed those practices which seem to express syncretism. They have been rightly suspicious of syncretizing tendencies because they imply that human creation can ultimately overcome (in the sense of Hegelian *Aufhebung*) what God has originally ordained and revealed.

7. GENERAL REVELATION AND SPECIAL REVELATION

Judaism and Christianity can jointly proclaim certain normative truths about the human condition—without the surrender demanded by proselytism, syncretism, or secularism—by affirming what Jewish and Christian traditions have taught about general revelation. The latter is historically antecedent to the special revelation each community, respectively, claims as its own basic norm. General revelation still functions even after that special revelation has occurred. For Jews, it is the affirmation of the revelation to the children of Noah, something which extends beyond the revelation to the children of Israel at Sinai.[18] For Roman Catholics and some Anglicans, it is the affirmation of natural law, something which extends beyond the divine law.[19] For many Protestants, certainly those of Lutheran or Reformed background, it is the affirmation of the order of creation, which extends beyond the gospel.[20] In all these traditions, it needs to be added, what is "beyond" is certainly not what is "higher" on any scale of value. Quite the contrary, what is more general is lower on that scale, a point that Jews who affirm the divine election of Israel, and Christians who affirm the incarnation, can readily understand. Nevertheless, what is more general and therefore lower is not without any value at all.

This general revelation, which makes itself manifest in certain universal moral principles, is most immediately accessible to human reason. It does not require a covenantal experience wherefrom the religious community proclaims it to the world. General revelation must be discovered within ordinary human experience. It must be seen from within that experience, as creating conditions necessary for authentic human community to be sustained. Yet the religious communities do not dissolve into some general human moral community by affirming these moral principles.

They must insist all along that these principles, though *necessary* for authentic human community, are not at all *sufficient* for authentic human fulfillment. That can only be commanded through revelation and consummated by salvation: the ultimate redemption of the world by its creator God.

Although the religious communities of Judaism and Christianity should not legislate this minimal human morality (indeed, when they do they most often retard its social impact, especially in a democracy), they do provide it with an overall ontological context, which is a continuing vision of its original grounds and its ultimate horizon. Without that continuing vision, the very operation of human moral reason, indeed all human reason itself, flounders. Reason cannot flourish for long in an ontological vacuum, namely, in an otherwise absurd universe and in an otherwise aimless trajectory of human history.

The constitution of the relation between God's revealed law and universal moral law is an intellectual operation, conducted not only differently by the respective religious communities themselves, but even by adherents of different theological and philosophical tendencies within those communities. Nevertheless, recognition of the similarity of the problematic, coming as it does out of that which both communities accept as sacred scripture, i.e. the Hebrew Bible, can lead to a new mutuality. Such mutuality allows each community to maintain its own faith integrity in relationship with God, with the members of its own covenant, with the members of the most proximate religion (which I hold is, for Jews, Christianity), and with the world beyond.

The final requirement is that both communities respect with theological cogency the integrity of the secular order. In America, that means respect for the *novus ordo seculorum,* carefully distinguishing its legitimate moral claims from the illegitimate philosophical claims of those who would insist that secularism can be its only sufficient foundation.[21] This respect for the integrity of the secular order, therefore, requires Jews and Christians to eschew those ultra-traditionalist elements in either community which wish to simply annul modernity *in toto* and return to their nostalgic vision of a theocratic polity of some sort or other. Both Jews and Christians should learn from modern history that the only means now available for such a restoration of any *ancien régime* come from fascism in its various guises—the most hideous caricature of the kingdom of God.

Whether the possibility of this new Jewish-Christian relationship will be realized in and for our time will depend in large measure on the theological ingenuity, philosophical perspicacity, and historical insight of leading thinkers in each community. For the most part, their work, both separately and in concert, still lies before them.

NOTES

1. *Mishnah: Abot* 5.22.

2. The various Jewish sources alluded to in this paper have been discussed in considerable detail in two books of mine: *The Image of the Non-Jew in Judaism: An Historical and Constructive Study of the Noahide Laws* (New York and Toronto, 1983); and *Jewish-Christian Dialogue: A Jewish Justification* (New York, 1989). Readers interested in studying these sources are referred to these two books. This paper is an attempt to recapitulate some of the main conclusions of these two books, and to express them in a way more relevant to the current situation of Jews and Christians in post-modern America.

3. Thus the great German Jewish thinker Hermann Cohen (d. 1918) wrote: "It is impossible to develop a unifying concept of Judaism unless the concept of Judaism itself is anticipated as an ideal project. . . . However, history by itself does not determine anything about the essence and peculiarity of the concept, which, in the course of history up to now, may not yet have developed to its final realization." *Religion of Reason Out of the Sources of Judaism,* trans. S. Kaplan (New York, 1972), p. 3.

4. See the classic study of Marcel Simon, *Verus Israel* (Paris, 1964), esp. pp. 165ff.

5. See D. Novak, "The Treatment of Muslims and Islam in the Legal Writings of Maimonides," in *Studies in the Islamic and Jewish Traditions,* ed. W.M. Brinner and S.D. Ricks (Chico, 1986), pp. 233ff.

6. See J. Habermas, *The Theory of Communicative Action: Reason and the Rationalization of Society,* trans. T. McCarthy (Boston, 1984), p. 398; also, *Knowledge and Human Interest,* trans. J.J. Shapiro (Boston, 1971), p. 137. Habermas has shown quite precisely how true communication as dialogue is not one side arguing the other side into its own pre-conceived theoretical position, but is rather a *praxis,* wherein both sides together contribute and develop their own intersubjective reality. He calls this process "sociation."

7. See Jacob Katz, *Exclusiveness and Tolerance* (Oxford, 1961), pp. 156ff.

8. Thus the statement of Vatican Council II in *Nostra Aetate* is perfectly cogent Christian theology. "Although the church is the new people of God, the Jews should not be presented as repudiated or cursed by God. . . ." *The Documents of Vatican II,* trans. ed. J. Gallagher (London and Dublin, 1966), p. 666. While this statement can be and indeed has been a highly effective instrument for bringing about more benevolent Catholic attitudes and actions involving Jews, it is still not sufficient for grounding actual Jewish-Christian dialogue. It need not, indeed cannot, be eliminated by Catholics in good faith with the magisterium of

their church, but it needs to be supplemented by philosophical and historical reflection.

9. The point of Christian derivation from Judaism as not only historical (hence surpassed) but ontological (hence continual) has been most forcefully and consistently argued by the contemporary Protestant theologian Paul van Buren. He writes: "The church's claim to relationship with Israel's God depends on Israel's prior relationship, for that alone provided the historically essential context for the existence of the one Israelite through whom the church has a claim to sonship. We must say more than this, however. Israel remains today the foundation of the church's claim to sonship." *A Theology of the Jewish-Christian Reality* (San Francisco, 1980), 1:80 (see 132, 156). Nevertheless, one must raise this question: According to van Buren's own theological criteria, could it not be reasonably inferred that the best way for Christians to identify with Jesus the Jew is for them to become Jews like Jesus himself, as van Buren puts it, "to join them [the Jews] on their own Halachic terms"? Ibid. p. 65. I raise this question because, ironically it might seem, my *Jewish* theological approach in dealing with Christianity, both in its premises and in its conclusions, does not in any way call for anything like Christian conversion or subordination to Judaism.

10. See Immanuel Kant, *Groundwork of the Metaphysic of Morals,* trans. H.J. Paton (New York, 1964), pp. 95ff.

11. John Courtney Murray, *We Hold These Truths: Catholic Reflections on the American Proposition* (New York, 1960), p. 19.

12. For MacIntyre on this subject, see *Whose Justice? Which Rationality?* (Notre Dame, 1988), esp. pp. 334ff; also, *After Virtue: A Study in Moral Theory* (Notre Dame, 1981), pp. 49ff. Along similar lines, see J. Stout, *The Flight From Authority: Religion, Morality and the Quest for Autonomy* (Notre Dame, 1981), pp. 62ff; Stanley Hauerwas, *A Community of Character: Toward A Constructive Christian Social Ethics* (Notre Dame, 1981), pp. 214–219.

13. Thomas Kuhn, *The Structure of Scientific Revolutions* (University of Chicago, 1970).

14. See D. Novak, "American Jews and America: The Mission of Israel Revisited," in *Jews in Unsecular America,* ed. Richard John Neuhaus (Grand Rapids, 1987), pp. 41ff.

15. For a fuller discussion of this specific issue, see Mary Ann Glendon, *Abortion and Divorce in Western Law* (Cambridge, 1987), pp. 119–134.

16. According to the Masoretic punctuation of this verse, it reads, "He made us and we are his." I have translated here the consonantal text. The use of both readings is actually complementary (which is not usually the case; see, e.g., *Babylonian Talmud:Sanhedrin* 4a–b). Clearly, if God made us and not we ourselves, then we belong to God and not to ourselves.

17. See Richard John Neuhaus, *The Naked Public Square: Religion and Democracy in America* (Grand Rapids, 1984), pp. 3ff.

18. In the Talmud, it was assumed that the full Torah contains the Noahide law and greatly surpasses it as well. See *Babylonian Talmud: Yebamot* 22a; *Sanhedrin*

59a. In fact, one can see the Noahide law as the *conditio sine qua non* of the Mosaic law, and the Mosaic law as the *conditio per quam* of the Noahide law. See Maimonides, *Mishneh Torah: Hilkhot Melakhim,* 9.1. In the following two notes, one can see that the Catholic theologian, Thomas Aquinas, and the Protestant theologian, John Calvin, said much the same thing, *mutatis mutandis,* in terms of the relation between general and special revelation in their respective traditions.

19. Note: "The natural law directs man by way of certain general precepts, common to both the perfect and the imperfect. Hence it is one and the same for all. But the divine law directs man also in certain particular matters, to which the perfect and imperfect do not share in the same relation." Thomas Aquinas, *Summa Theologiae,* 2-1, q. 91, a. 5, ad 3, trans. in *The Basic Writings of St. Thomas Aquinas,* ed. A. Pegis (New York, 1945), 2:755. Also, note: "[It] is not that whatever is contained in the Law and the Gospel belongs to the natural law, since they contain many things that are above nature; but that whatever belongs to the natural law is fully contained in them." *Ibid.,* q. 94, a. 4, ad 1 (2:778).

20. Note: "It is a fact that the law which we call the moral law is nothing else than a testimony of natural law and of that conscience which God has engraved upon the minds of men." John Calvin, *Institutes of the Christian Religion,* 4.20.16, trans. F.L. Battles (Philadelphia, 1960), 2:1504. Also, note: "Nay, even for the children of God, before they are called and while they are destitute of the Spirit of sanctification. . . . It is profitable for them to undergo this tutelage. . . . As a consequence, when they are called, they are not utterly untutored and uninitiated in discipline as if it were something unknown." Ibid. 2.7.10 (1:359).

21. Murray, *We Hold These Truths,* p. 56.

A Jewish View of Christianity

Michael Wyschogrod

In the last forty or so years, several dozen Christian bodies have adopted statements about Jewish-Christian relations. It is widely conceded that this concentration of attention on the Jewish issue by Christian bodies is largely the result of the Holocaust. It is possible that even without the Holocaust, Christian interest in Judaism would have escalated in the closing decades of the twentieth century. The maturation of the historical method made it more and more difficult to overlook the deeply Jewish character of early Christianity. So even without the Holocaust, it is not unlikely that Christian scholarship would have been forced to deal more seriously with the Jewish roots of Christianity.

But this was not to be. The Holocaust occurred, and instead of an organic development prompted by scholarly and theological considerations, a world historical evil event of unprecedented proportions intervened and cast Jewish-Christian relations, and many other things, in an entirely new light. The Christian side in the dialogue found itself burdened with a heavy guilt. While Nazism was hardly a Christian phenomenon, there was widespread agreement that two thousand years of the Christian teaching of contempt prepared the ground for the "final solution." Christianity was forced to face up to the implications of its teaching which were taken to insane extremes by the Nazis but which also built on Christian foundations.

On its side, Judaism entered the dialogue in the post-World War II period in a seriously weakened position. The Holocaust was, of course, the deepest reason for the weakening. No people could suffer the fate European Jewry did without showing signs of deep trauma. But the trauma the Holocaust inflicted on world Jewry must be understood in the context of Jewish history since the enlightenment. This history, in turn, must be viewed in the context of Jewish self-understanding rooted in the doctrine of election and the Jewish self-image that this doctrine generates. The product resulting from the interaction of these influences yielded a deeply injured Judaism that embarked on Jewish-Christian dialogue after World War II.

DEFEAT AND SECULARISM

When we consider the three monotheistic religions—Judaism, Christianity and Islam—we can conclude that of the three, Judaism and Islam have been wounded religions and Christianity much less so. Islam, from its inception, has seen itself validated by its early success. Starting out as the faith of a small group of believers on the Arabian peninsula, the message of Islam quickly conquered vast territories that were brought under Moslem hegemony by means of both the book and the sword. Islam's success validated the faith as nothing else could, an attitude not unknown to either Judaism or Christianity. Religions often interpret worldly success as a sign of divine favor but this is perhaps more deeply rooted in Islam than in the other two monotheistic religions. The existence of a political realm in which Islam is supreme is thus essential to the spiritual health of Islam, largely because of Islam's refusal to separate the religious from the political. The existence of territories where Islam has not yet succeeded in establishing its authority can only be interpreted as a temporary state of affairs to be remedied at the earliest possible moment.

It is for this reason that European imperialism of the nineteenth century was so profoundly painful to Islam. By the end of the century, the Moslem world was largely subordinate to the power of Christian Europe. Largely due to the superiority of western science—but not only for that reason—the Moslem world found itself deprived of its sovereignty or reduced to the status of vassal states of European Christian powers that had set out to establish empires in Africa and Asia.

How could this happen to Islam, the true faith that was destined to rule the world and to unite all of humanity under the banner of the teaching of the prophet? Failure of such magnitude after so much success was also unbearable because Islam never embraced suffering as a desirable part of the religious life. Where suffering could not be avoided, a highly detailed doctrine of other-worldly rewards rushed in to take the sting out of the suffering and to assure the faithful that the suffering was as nothing compared to the assured reward.

Since the advent of the age of imperialism until the defeats suffered in the Arab-Israeli conflict, Islam has been a wounded faith that has had great difficulty in coming to terms with its relatively weak position in a world that should have yielded long ago to the message of the one true religion. The wounds imposed on Islam manifest themselves in various ways among which fanaticism and the development of denial mechanisms are the most prominent. Such manifestations can also be observed in contemporary Judaism.

The injuries suffered by Islam are of interest because they enable us to understand better the injuries suffered by Judaism. Moslems see themselves as followers of the last and the greatest of the prophets whose revelation is God's final message to humanity. Jews see themselves as members of a people chosen by God for special proximity and service to him. While God loves all of his children, he has a special love for the people of Israel, particularly when that people is faithful to him and obeys his commandments. But even when it does not—and it frequently has not—God's undeserved love for the people of his election is not erased but only temporarily suspended. After God's anger passes, the original love returns, perhaps in increased measure. Like the love of a parent for an erring child, God's affection for Israel is indestructible. It is the expression of God's eternal faithfulness.

If this is so, then why does Israel suffer so much? Why does Israel live in exile, despised and persecuted everywhere? Is this the fate appropriate to the chosen people? These are questions Jews have asked over the centuries and with particular vehemence since the Holocaust. Since there are no satisfactory answers to these questions, a certain spiritual injury has taken up abode in the Jewish soul. And it is an injury which, we will see, injects itself into the Jewish-Christian dialogue.

It is, of course, not the case that there are no answers at all to these questions. Traditionally, Jewish suffering has been explained as the result of sin. When Israel is faithful to the covenant, all goes well, and when it is not, all sorts of calamities befall the people (for the biblical source of this idea see Deut 11:13–17). On the frequent occasions that calamities did occur, the standard explanation was the sin of the people. This left the traditional system intact and held out the promise of improvement if the people improved their ways.

The messianic idea was an integral part of this system. Given Israel's sense of election, its particular closeness to God and God's profound faithfulness to Israel, no defeat of Israel could be final. However final the defeat seemed, it could only be a temporary reversal. God would redeem his people from exile. God would reestablish the destroyed kingdom and Israel would dwell safely in its homeland once again. Messianic redemption was the expectation that would not die because the current situation of exile could not last forever. God will fulfill his promises to his chosen people.

When truly accepted, this system of beliefs did much to shield Israel from deep psychic and spiritual injury. Persecution was a sign of election, of the jealousy and hatred of the nations who could not accept Israel's special status and rebelled against God's sovereign election of Israel. While Jews rarely turned suffering into something inherently desirable, they learned to accept it because they were convinced of its non-permanence and that, by changing their ways, their situation would change for the better.

Gradually, however, this system of beliefs began to be eroded. A number of factors contributed to this. First, there was the length and severity of the exile. For how long can a situation be termed temporary? How much suffering is compatible with the conviction that it is an expression of God's passing anger, soon to be replaced by the returning love of a temporarily angered parent-God? Could it be that God's love for Israel was much less intense than had been believed or perhaps even non-existent? Such questions were, until recent times, rarely permitted to enter Jewish consciousness. But even below the conscious level, they could do much damage.

And then there was, of course, the crisis of modernization. The secularization that swept over Europe during the enlightenment had an immense impact on European Jewry. It undermined in large measure the theological worldview that has been outlined. But that is only the beginning because secularization was not the exclusive enterprise of Jews. With the French Revolution, much of Europe began a process of secularization. For Jews, the enlightenment was experienced as the beginning of the end of exclusion.

For Jews as for no others, secularization was not a cultural-historical phenomenon connected with the end of the middle ages and the rise of science but a development that promised to end the exclusion of the Jews from the cultural and economic life of Europe. The fact that medieval civilization had been deeply Christian accounted for this exclusion. Suddenly the prospect of a de-Christianized Europe opened up, and it is not difficult to understand that many Jews seized this prospect as the beginning of Jewish liberation. Citizens would no longer be Jews or Christians but members of the human race. The faculty of reason would unite all of humanity.

There was a price to be paid for this liberation, however. It consisted of a weakening if not an abandonment of Jewish identity. Here is the source of the deep attraction to secularism that is inherent in modern Judaism. This tendency was, of course, much more pronounced among western Jews. The Jews of eastern Europe continued to live in a largely pre-modern society. But even there, the *haskalah,* the Jewish version of the enlightenment, began to assert itself and had not the Holocaust intervened, it would undoubtedly have changed the orientation of eastern Jewry in a secular direction.

In summary, then, Judaism, like Islam, found itself injured even before the period of the Holocaust. While the enlightenment seemed to promise an abatement of Jewish suffering, this did not materialize and the Holocaust proved once and for all that the dangers for Jews in the modern period were not smaller but greater than before. It became more and more difficult, especially after the Holocaust, to sustain the doctrine of the chosenness of Israel. When we add to this the fact that many Jews experienced secularization as the price of admission into European society, we cannot evade the conclusion that the Judaism that entered into dialogue with Christianity after World War II was a seriously weakened version of the faith.

What was the condition of Christianity? It, too, was weakened but not as much as Judaism or Islam. Like Islam, Christianity had originally also been an incredible success story. Unlike Judaism and Islam, Christianity had never been defeated by a civilization expressive of another faith. It was, of course, weakened by secularization and various schisms, particularly the reformation, but Christianity never had to ask itself why Christians are living under the oppression of Jews or Moslems. It was the west that was ruling the world, and even if the west was not doing this altogether in the name of Christianity, the fact that western civilization and its technology became the dominant influence in the modern world did nothing to undermine Christianity's self-confidence.

Other than the growth of secularism, Christianity in the twentieth century was seriously threatened by left- and right-wing totalitarianism. For the first time since Constantine, there were countries in Europe ruled by explicitly anti-Christian regimes. This was perfectly clear in the Soviet Union and its post-World War II satellites, but it was also partly true in

Nazi Germany where an ideology ruled that was anti-Christian even if not as explicitly so as Marxist totalitarianism.

The Holocaust was a trauma for Christianity because it made visible the possibility of a non-Christian or even anti-Christian transmutation of Christian antisemitism, more virulent even than the original form. Nevertheless, these post-Christian forms of antisemitism were seen by many to owe much to Christian antisemitism, and that is the reality Christianity now had to face.

ORTHODOX JUDAISM AND DIALOGUE

With this background in mind, I now move to our actual topic: a contemporary Jewish view of Christianity. My focus will not be on the historical aspect, though history cannot be eschewed altogether. But history must not be permitted to reign unchallenged. The temptation to do so is very great. History is a convenient way of escaping the necessity for taking a position. Ever since the middle of the nineteenth century and the advent of "Wissenschaft des Judentums," the "scientific" study of Judaism, an atmosphere was generated as if Judaism had only a past but no present or future. Yet the "scientific" study of the past was possible only because in the past there were people who were making Judaism happen. If all we do now is study the past of Judaism, those who come after us will have nothing to study but detailing the way in which we looked at the past—in other words, writing a history of the way we wrote history.

The issue, then, is how today's Jews view today's Christians. But the Judaism of today is a fragmented entity. The fact is that a significant portion of Judaism, namely the Orthodox branch, refuses to engage in any dialogue with Christianity. For many Orthodox Jews, Christianity is a foreign religion with which Jews should have as little to do as possible. From the point of view of right-wing Orthodoxy, dialogue with Christianity can only lead to a blurring of the division between the two faiths, and to Jewish conversion. The first priority of Orthodox Judaism is the preservation of the Jewish people as the people who observe the Torah. In the modern world this requires building very prominent fences around Jews who are characterized in the Bible as "a people that dwells apart" (Num 23:9). Since this even requires separation from non-Orthodox Jews, how much more so from non-Jews. The result of this is that the Israeli chief-rabbinate, the leadership of the Israeli and American Yeshiva world, and the other organizations that speak for right-wing Orthodoxy exclude themselves completely from the Jewish-Christian dialogue. While this does not, technically speaking, constitute a theological evaluation of Christianity, it is, in fact, even worse than a negative theological evaluation. There is nothing as bad, in my mind, as the refusal to speak with the other. Where there is communication there is hope, but where there is no communication, the very basis of hope is absent.

Left-wing Orthodoxy, the Orthodoxy that does not reject modernity but tries to combine faithful Torah observance with secular education and participation in the professions, takes a more complex stand with regard to dialogue with Christianity. In an article that appeared in the Spring-Summer 1964 issue of *Tradition* published by the Rabbinical Council of America, Rabbi Joseph B. Soloveitchik laid down the guidelines on Jewish-Christian dialogue that are widely accepted by modern Orthodox Jews.

Soloveitchik says: "We have always considered ourselves an inseparable part of humanity . . . committed to the general welfare and progress of mankind," and "We are interested in combating disease, in alleviating human suffering, in protecting man's rights, in helping the needy, *et cetera*. . . ." Because this is so, we are prepared to deal with Christianity with respect to the secular problems that we both face. "In the secular sphere," he writes, "we may discuss positions to be taken, ideas to be evolved, and plans to be formulated. In these matters, religious communities may together recommend action to be developed and may seize the initiative to be implemented later by general society."

But, continues Soloveitchik, "it is important that the religious or theological *logos* should not be employed as the medium of communication between two faith communities whose modes of expression are as unique as their apocalyptic experiences." "The word of faith," Soloveitchik insists, "reflects the intimate, the private, the paradoxically inexpressible cravings of the individual for and his linking up with the Maker. It reflects the luminous character and the strangeness of the act of faith of a particular community which is totally incomprehensible to the man of a different faith community." He adds: "As a matter of fact, our common interests lie not in the realm of faith, but in that of the secular order."

Having said this, Soloveitchik reveals his understanding of the weakness of his case by remarking in a footnote: "The term 'secular orders' is used here in accordance with its popular semantics. For the man of faith, this term is a misnomer. God claims the whole, not a part of man, and whatever He establishes as an order within the scheme of creation is sacred."

This, of course, is the crux of the matter. Soloveitichik requires that when Orthodox Jews enter into dialogue with Christians, they do so as human beings and not as Jews. There exists a neutral realm in which Jews and Christians can interact without their religious commitments having to play any role. In this neutral realm, questions of social policy, such as war and peace, poverty and medical-ethical issues can be discussed. But it is essential that no religious or theological topics be raised because the religious "reflects the intimate, the private, the paradoxically inexpressible cravings of the individual for and his linking up with his Maker." These matters are so private that they cannot be shared or, at the very least, should not be shared, almost as if sharing them constituted a form of voyeurism that Soloveitchik finds unacceptable.

But how would such a Jewish-Christian dialogue function in which the participants were determined to exclude their religious commitments? Suppose the discussion turned to abortion, to take one example. Could the Jewish side discuss this without taking into account the halachic stand on this issue? Should the Jewish side pretend that it is approaching this question and other similar questions purely from a secular, rational point of view, uninfluenced by the written and oral Torahs which are documents of revelation accepted in faith? And the very same will be true of Christians. Many Christian attitudes to social and ethical issues are deeply rooted in the standpoint of Christian faith. Were this not the case, both Jewish and Christian faiths would be irrelevant to the issues that agitate a troubled humanity. Both of these faiths fuse the religious with the secular. In any case, Judaism does in a marked way.

Soloveitchik is, of course, aware of this, and it is for this reason that he inserts the footnote, previously noted, in which he writes that the term "secular orders," as used in his statement that "our common interests lie not in the realm of faith, but in that of the secular orders," is a misnomer. "God claims," he writes, "the whole, not a part of man, and whatever He established as an order within the scheme of creation is sacred." So the world does not come divided into a "secular" and a "religious" realm, and the participants in Jewish-Christian dialogue must react not only as secular but also as religious persons.

Because it is clear that Soloveitchik understood all of this, a slightly Machiavellian interpretation of his position suggests itself. Right-wing Orthodoxy, as we have seen, opposes all dialogue, indeed almost all contact, with Christians and other non-Jews. Soloveitchik does not share this isolationism. As a western educated person, he believes that contact with western culture is permissible and even desirable, and this includes contact with the churches. But he had to cover his right flank, and in order to do so, he invented this theory of bifurcated dialogue. Religious topics may not be discussed because they are too private but social and ethical topics may be. It seems possible that he understood quite clearly that the distinction is not defensible, that once dialogue begins with ethical and social issues, the religious and theological plane will quickly be reached. If I am correct, this was his prudent way of approving something for which he could have been criticized severely by the Right had he not veiled his position to some degree. In other words, this would be another instance of *Persecution and the Art of Writing*, to quote the title of Leo Strauss' essay about writers who are forced to disguise their true meaning but leave hints so that an elite will be able to discover their real teaching.

Nevertheless, American modern Orthodoxy has adhered to the surface meaning of Soloveitchik's guidelines. Wherever they have been able to exert their influence (as in the Synagogue Council of America) they have seen to it that the dialogue avoided theological issues. This has inhibited the development of a theological dialogue and has particularly inhibited the formation of a Jewish theology of Christianity.

TRINITY AND INCARNATION

As in ages past, the most difficult problem the Jew faces when viewing Christianity is the topic of christology. In Judaism and Islam, the highest level a human being can reach is that of prophet. Unlike the philosopher, the prophet does not teach a truth he has discovered by means of reason, but he teaches a truth or message committed to him by God for transmission to humanity. The question whether a particular person was or was not a true prophet is, of course, one of great importance. It is the question that separates Judaism from Islam. Judaism does not accept Mohammed as a prophet, particularly not as the greatest of the prophets, while Islam does. Significant as this disagreement is, it pales to insignificance when compared to the disagreement between Judaism and Christianity about the divinity of Jesus. A prophet is a human being chosen by God to transmit his message to humanity. The contention that Jesus was both fully human and fully divine blurs, from the Jewish point of view, the difference between God and man and therefore raises the possibility of idolatry.

Because our orientation here is not primarily historical, we will make no pretense of surveying Jewish comments about the Trinity and the incarnation. We need only note that all Jewish writers have expressed varying degrees of disagreement with these doctrines. The only question left open was whether these doctrines turn Christianity into an idolatrous religion, a category with serious implications for Jewish law. The majority opinion seems to have been that Christianity is not idolatry, particularly for non-Jews. This is based on the perhaps curious idea that the precise definition of what constitutes idolatry is not the same for Jews as for Gentiles. It becomes more understandable when we remember that, from the rabbinic point of view, different legal requirements apply to Jews and non-Jews.

While recognizing the intractability of this problem in the past, what about the present and the future? Can we hope for any progress, for a narrowing of the gap, for a reduction of the intensity of the disagreement? Is such a hope desirable? Is it not best to accept the reality of the disagreement and to leave it at that?

I would argue with conviction that such a non-interventionist policy is religiously unacceptable in this situation. The necessity for dialogue even about such issues as the Trinity and the incarnation is rooted in religious reality. If I, as a Jew, believe that the Trinity and the incarnation are false doctrines that either border on or constitute idolatry, then it is my duty as a Jew to persuade my Christian friends to abandon these teachings. Non-Jews are required to adhere to the so-called Noahide commandments based on Genesis 9:1–7, one of which prohibits idolatry. The only remaining question then is whether Jews have a responsibility to teach the Noahide commandments to Gentiles. Since it is difficult to see where else but from Jews Gentiles could obtain information about the Noahide commandments, it seems reasonable to conclude that Jews have a responsibility to teach to Gentiles the Noahide commandments, including the prohibition against idolatry.

But there is more. The natural tendency has been for Jews to view Christianity as a foreign faith whose otherness is nowhere displayed more clearly than in the teachings of the Trinity and the incarnation. Focusing exclusively on the discontinuity between the two faiths, Judaism and Christianity have become more and more estranged, with little effort on either side to supplement the element of discontinuity with the significant dimensions of continuity that must not be ignored. Some Jewish authors in the past have recognized the positive role Christianity has played in God's redemptive plan, but even they have not found any positive elements in the Trinity and the incarnation, the teachings which Judaism finds most difficult to understand.

The effect has been a kind of polarization. The more Christianity has moved in an incarnational direction, the more Judaism moved in a transcendental direction. The divine and human natures, Judaism insists, are very different. God is above any human categories of understanding. Biblical anthropomorphism does not mean what it says. God is an absolute who is above time and space, and no attributes can be attached to him. In short, there has been a tendency to transform the God of the Bible into the God of the philosophers.

I am firmly convinced that this does not constitute a service to Judaism. I am not arguing that this tendency in Judaism is solely the result of a recoil from Christian ideas. But it is at least partly that, and we have here a situation in which both faiths have damaged one another. It seems to me that just as Judaism recoiled from the Trinity and the incarnation toward a non-biblical absolute rather than to the personal God of the Bible, so Christianity responded to the Jewish rejection of Jesus as the messiah by raising him to the status of a divine being co-equal in his divinity to that of the Father who sent him.

All this was possible because the God of the Hebrew Bible was depicted as harboring within himself two divergent characteristics. On the one hand is the absolute dimension. He is not merely one God among many, but the only God. Even if there are other beings with superhuman powers, the God of Israel is more powerful than any of them. There is no limit to his power; in effect, he can do anything. While there is relatively little in the Hebrew Bible that makes God out to be omniscient (at times, he seems surprised by developments he did not anticipate), his knowledge is clearly greater than that of humans, and the lack of omniscience might even be interpreted as a self-imposed limitation. In short, the God of the Hebrew Bible is so overwhelmingly powerful that absolutist claims about him seem to have considerable biblical support.

At the same time, the biblical God is also very human. The Bible has no difficulty depicting God as a personality interacting with human beings. He has emotions, needs, desires, disappointments. He can be influenced, positively and negatively. He seems to profit from experience. He has his likes and dislikes and sometimes he develops a particular affection for an individual or a group. But he also gets angry at those he loves when they do not obey him, and when he does, he can be very punitive. However his anger generally passes and then the love returns. Very often he is best understood as a parent whose love for his child waxes and wanes as the conduct of the child varies.

These two dimensions of God are not easy to hold in balance. It is easiest to choose one of the two dimensions as primary, with the other not to be taken too seriously. Maimonides, within Judaism, focuses on the absolutist dimension and expends a great amount of energy to explain away the anthropomorphic passages in the Bible. That is, however, rather an exception. Most Jews, ancient or medieval (Rashi would be an example of the latter), had no great difficulty with the problem of anthropomorphism, but they certainly did have difficulty with the doctrine of incarnation.

The doctrine that one of the three persons constituting God became incarnate in the body of the Jew from Nazareth is thus a particular sharpening of divine personalism. The humanity of God is transposed from an anthropomorphic way of speaking about God which, it is understood, is not to be taken fully literally, to an ontological assertion that God actually *became* man, that the divine and human natures were blended in at least one case into one personality with two natures. Needless to say, this is deeply troubling to Jewish ears even if we keep in mind that the transcendental aspect of God is preserved, in a fashion, by maintaining that God the Father does not participate in the incarnation. Were this not the case, were Christianity to have taught that there is a non-triune God who became incarnated in the body of a human being, the break with Jewish sensibilities would have been even more profound.

So the teaching of the triune and incarnated God remains a source of deep difficulty between Judaism and Christianity. It is incumbent upon Jews to deal with this teaching. It is a teaching not difficult to caricature, and Jews have not missed the opportunity to do so. But many teachings can be caricatured, and it behooves Jews to ask themselves whether interpretations of these doctrines can be developed that would make them less objectionable to Jews. Chances are that such less objectionable interpretations might be more faithful to the Christian message than interpretations which make the gulf with Judaism as great as possible.

By the time of Nicea, the church had very little interest in how Jews would react to any particular doctrine. If anything, a negative Jewish reaction recommended a teaching because it strengthened Christian as against Jewish identity. This may have changed now. For Christians the views of Jews cannot and should not be decisive in determining the soundness of any particular teaching. But perhaps the time has come when a negative Jewish reaction is no longer a recommendation. All things being equal, many Christians today believe that a version of Christianity which reduces the gulf toward Judaism may be preferable and more authentic. In that spirit, dialogue about the Trinity and the incarnation—the most difficult issues between the two faiths—may be of advantage to all concerned.

TORAH

The Trinity and the incarnation are the very first topics contemporary Jews see in regard to Christianity. Second is Christianity's view of the Torah. It has been said that Christianity teaches salvation through Jesus Christ, all man and all God, while Judaism teaches salvation through obedience to the Torah of Moses. There is an element of truth in this, though it is probably not accurate to speak of Judaism as teaching salvation by any means, including the Torah of Moses. A religion does not teach salvation unless it sees man posed between salvation and perdition, with the latter likely in the absence of some extraordinary intervention. While punishments of various sorts, including some very severe ones, are not unknown in Judaism, the stark options of salvation or perdition in the other-worldly sense are not at the center of thinking. In that sense, Judaism is not a salvational religion.

Nevertheless, the Torah plays a central role in the Judaism that evolved after the destruction of the temple in 70 C.E. It played a central role before the destruction of the temple as well. The service in the temple, the roles of the priests and the Levites, and many other details were all regulated by the commandments of the Torah. But with the destruction of the temple the Torah came to occupy an even more central role. It was God's guidance to Israel, cleaving to which meant eternal life for the people and abandoning of which meant disaster. The Torah became the portable temple which Jews could carry into exile and by means of which they remained attached to the God who had chosen them. It was the lifeline of the Jewish people to God.

Over the ages, most Jews have experienced Christianity as a deadly assault on the Torah. The truth of the matter is, of course, much more complex and the complexity of the Christian position is the source of hope for the future. But we must start with the uncomplex truth that Christianity is an assault on the Torah, at least as Jews have understood and lived the Torah.

For Jews, the Torah is the expression of God's will for the conduct of the Jewish people. It is not only that. It is the telling of the stories that collectively constitute the history and self-understanding of the Jewish people. Also, an essential part of the Torah comprises the commandments which Israel takes very seriously. They deal with all imaginable areas of life, from the spiritual to the most mundane, and Israel tries, to the best of its abilities, to obey them.

Juxtaposed against this view is the Christian view—or what many consider the Christian view—of the Torah as a law of death. The Torah bestows death because it bestows guilt. Nobody can live up to the demands of the Torah, and when man violates its commandments—which he inevitably does—then the result is catastrophe. Instead of being a gift of love, then, the Torah is a trap, a Trojan horse which appears at first sight as a divine gift but which really turns out to be a potent poison that causes the painful death of those who place their trust in it.

Those who place their trust in the Torah are, of course, the Jews who have paid dearly for their foolish confidence in the works of the law. Christians place their trust in Jesus and are saved because they know that faith saves and law condemns. As long as they lack faith, Jews will be condemned by the very Torah whose commandments they adhere to without any profit.

If this is an accurate summary of the Christian view of Torah, then the Jewish view of Christianity cannot be a very positive one. This is true even though many Jews since the enlightenment no longer obey the commandments of the Torah in the comprehensive way of Jews in the past. Liberal Judaism, deeply committed to an historical and evolutionary view of Judaism, has discarded some of the pentateuchal commandments as time-bound and no longer significant for the contemporary Jew. From a certain perspective, liberal Judaism's freedom with the law could be interpreted as drawing closer to the Christian view. If Christianity early on proclaimed that all foods are permitted, then liberal Judaism came to that conclusion in the nineteenth century. So at least non-Orthodox Jews finally came to agree with at least part of Christian teaching, even if not the most central part.

But there is less here than meets the eye. Christianity's critical attitude to the law is based on the conviction that the law results in guilt rather than salvation. Liberal Judaism's, on the other hand, is based on the view that the law is largely a human creation that shows the marks of the age in which it originated. Many portions of the law, it is thought, are not divine in origin and can therefore be modified or even cancelled. The essence of God's will, according to liberal Judaism, is expressed in the moral rather than cultic law. So while it is true that liberal Judaism shares with Christianity flexibility with respect to the law, the reasons for the flexibility are quite different, and not too much should be made of the common flexibility.

If the Christian view of the law as a law of death remains in force, then the estrangement between Christianity and Judaism will prevail. Fortunately, there is reason to believe that the Christian view as I have expounded it is at least incomplete. Starting with the New Testament (e.g. Mt 5:17–20), there are passages which speak very positively about the law. The key to the matter is Christianity's acceptance of the Old Testament as the word of God. However much significance is attached to the new covenant as transforming and fulfilling the old, the fact remains that God speaks not only in the New but also in the Old Testament and that his commandments there were a valid expression of God's will at least for a time.

Over the centuries, Christian debate about the law has revolved around the before-Jesus and after-Jesus axis. The idea was that the law was in full effect before the coming of Jesus, but that with his coming, large parts of it were suspended. The problem then was which parts were declared inoperative and which not. This question was never answered with the requisite clarity, though not a few Christian authors have tried.

There is yet another way of looking at the problem which may be more productive for Jewish-Christian relations. Jews have long believed that the full Mosaic law was binding only on Jews. Non-Jews were duty-bound to obey the Noahide commandments, and if they did so, God was fully pleased. The tendency was to discourage Gentiles from abandoning their Noahide obligations and entering the covenant of Israel. Life under the yoke of the commandments was not easy. Israel had often proven inadequate to the task and had to pay dearly for its failure. Why then subject Gentiles to this burden? Only if the Gentile insisted, contrary to all advice, to enter the covenant of Abraham was he accepted as a full Jew.

It seems that this problem played a crucial role in early Christianity. The Jerusalem church consisted of Jewish believers in Jesus of Nazareth, but soon Gentiles were attracted to the Jesus-believing community. Did these Gentiles require circumcision and full Torah-obedience, or could they be accepted as followers of Jesus while living in accordance with the Noahide commandments? It seems, judging from Acts 15, that the Jerusalem church was divided on this issue. One faction believed that Gentiles who wished to follow Jesus had to be circumcised and obey the Torah of the Jews, while the other faction required only faith in Jesus and obedience to the Noahide commandments. The latter group carried the day at the first Jerusalem council described in Acts 15.

It is quite clear, however, that both factions in Jerusalem agreed that Jews, even after Jesus, remained under the prescriptions of the Torah. If the Jesus event had changed Jewish Torah obligation, then it would hardly make any sense to argue whether non-Jews required circumcision and Torah obligation. The debate concerned Gentiles; both sides agreed about the Torah obligation of Jesus-believing Jews.

If all this is true, then it puts Paul's criticism of the law in a totally new light. Paul's letters in which he criticizes the law were written to Gentiles who were being influenced by Jewish Jesus-believers to accept circumcision and Torah observance. Paul wishes to persuade them that this is neither necessary nor desirable. In so doing, he emphasizes and even exaggerates all the disadvantages and dangers of living under the law. He carefully omits all the advantages of Israel's covenant under the Torah because he has a specific purpose in mind: to dissuade Gentile Jesus-believers from placing themselves under the obligations of the Torah. Were he writing to Jews, his evaluation of Torah observance would have been very different.

At present, this alternative reading of the early Christian attitude to the law is not widely accepted. Some Christian scholars seem to have sympathy for it, but they are in a minority. Still, much is at stake here. Jews cannot view with much sympathy a Christianity that adheres to the teaching of contempt for the Torah of Moses.

We have dealt with two of the crucial issues in the Jewish-Christian relationship: christology and the Torah. They are, of course, not the only outstanding problems between the two faiths, though they are probably the two most difficult ones. Of the two, christology seems to be the more intractable. On the Torah issue, I have proposed a direction which might make it possible for Christians to accept the obligatory nature of Torah commandments for Jews even after Jesus. Jews will continue to follow with deep interest the attitudes of Christians to these issues.

As Christians deepen their understanding of Christianity's Jewish roots, Jews must try to understand Christianity's role in God's redemptive work. In respectful dialogue, the estrangement of the past will be overcome.

A Personal Perspective on Christianity

S. Daniel Breslauer

THEOLOGY, DIALOGUE, AND A JEWISH PERSPECTIVE

A colleague of mine who teaches at a Catholic university was once confronted by a student confused by an apparent contradiction. "You seem an intelligent person," the student remarked. "Yet you still believe in Judaism. If you're intelligent, why aren't you a Christian?" I don't recall what my colleague responded. One obvious response, however, suggests that the student has answered his own question. Matters of religious faith and commitment spring not from intellectual understanding but from other sources of human knowing and learning. The past attitude of Christians to Jews has often ignored this fact of human religious faith. The expectation that dialogue will result in conversion to Christianity once Jews learn its intellectual cogency misunderstands the anthropology of how people develop and express their faiths. Such an approach, as Eugene Borowitz has suggested, is not merely ineffectual but an affront to a partner in dialogue. Borowitz goes further and claims that dialogue for the sake of conversion represents "a violation of the mutuality implicit in the covenant of conversation."[1]

The legacy of *Nostra Aetate,* however, moves beyond such misunderstandings in the past and stimulates genuine conversation. Edward Flannery, in this spirit, suggests a new goal for dialogue, not conversion but "the reconciliation of the Jewish and Christian peoples, considered in their entirety."[2] Peoples, as entireties, however, cannot speak to one another. Dialogue occurs between individual people, not between collectivities. If Jews and Christians are to respect each other's traditions, they must do so on the basis of personal dialogue.

That dialogue must begin by each partner taking the other seriously as an individual rather than as representative of a general type. Christians often fail to see the variety of options within Judaism and apply a stereotypical model derived either from New Testament texts or from popular misconceptions of "the Jew." Jewish thinkers often fall into the same trap by identifying Christianity with its earliest phases. Jesus serves to represent one form of Christian religion and Paul a second. Rarely do Jews investigate the medieval and modern developments of Christianity.[3]

This lack of communication between Jew and Christian sometimes stems not from misconceptions and stereotypes, but from an otherwise laudable intention: that of diplomatic politeness. Both Jews and Christians seek to overcome centuries of hostility and to embrace one another as valued friends. Jewish-Christian dialogue too frequently slips into a stylized type of interaction by avoiding substantive disagreement. Jews and Christians strive for civility, to portray themselves and their partners in dialogue in the best possible light; thus each stresses what the one can learn from the other. Such cordiality merits commendation, but it does not often illuminate the real differences separating the participants. Politeness, valuable as a means of creating a climate for interaction and mutual respect, falls short of true dialogue and conversation.

Michael A. Singer laments the tendency of dialogue partners to treat one another as honored host or honored guest, to interact on a formal level with the "ideal" types of Jew and Christian. He comments that such conversations consist of reactions by one party to another, not true dialogue. Unfortunately, he himself employs a stereotypical image by suggesting that "If Jacob and Esau are our biblical prototypes, we shall never be able to move to the resolution they experienced."[4] Using biblical images only reinforces stereotypes and prejudices.

The image of Jacob and Esau as reconciled siblings entails an ironic pessimism. The biblical brothers failed to reach reconciliation and concord. In Genesis 33:14 Jacob promises to rendezvous with Esau in Seir. That meeting, however, never comes to pass. Rav Abbahu, a leading Amoraitic teacher (279–320 C.E.) of Caesarea, popular with Jew and non-Jew alike, commented that he had reviewed the entire scripture and could find no mention of Jacob's coming to Seir. Could Jacob have really been a deceiver after all? Heaven forbid! He would keep his promise, but only in messianic times when "the delivered will ascend Mount Zion to judge the mountain of Esau (Mount Seir)" (Ob 1:21).[5] Both Jews and Christians share a rather imperialistic view of the messianic eschaton. Humanity will be united in a single worshiping community; unbelievers will repent of their ways and join the true faith. Such an eschatological "reconciliation" hardly seems a model for Jewish-Christian dialogue during this very historical period "in our times."

Rabbi Abbahu's interpretation of Genesis 33 implies that Jew and Christian will meet only when Israel finally triumphs over Edom at the end of time, not in this historical period of dialogue. That same Rav Abbahu, however, offers a very different paradigm for Jewish-Gentile dialogue. By example, he demonstrates how relationships between Jews and Christians, rather than the relation between a putative "Judaism" and a putative "Christianity," offer a useful model for understanding the place of Christianity within a theology of Judaism.

Abbahu's model for dialogue occurs within the context of Jewish-Gentile relationships generally in Greco-Roman times. The Talmud often refers to dialogues between Jews and Gentiles. The term frequently used for "Gentile" (*Minim*) often indicates Christian sectarians so that stories about such Gentiles may refer to conversations between Jews and Christians. Dialogue between Jew and non-Jew began in the earliest period of post-biblical Judaism. Hellenistic Jews explained their faith to their Greek-speaking friends; great rabbis, legend relates, held discussions with Roman emperors; wealthy non-Jews challenged rabbinic masters to decode the secrets of the Hebrew scriptures. Those Jews who showed their scholarly ability to non-Jews were highly respected.

In this vein, the Talmud tells how Rav Abbahu once commended Rav Safra to certain Gentiles as a scholar of religious lore. On the basis of this recommendation they treated Rav Safra with respect and honor. Once, however, these non-Jews approached the rabbi and asked him to explain the verse in Amos 3:2, "You only have I known among the nations, therefore will I visit all your iniquities upon you." Rav Safra was at a loss to explain the verse, and so the non-Jews subjected him to ridicule and persecution. Rav Abbahu happened by and was accused of having misled his friends. He assured them that they had not been misled; Rav Safra was indeed a learned Jew, but Jews are not accustomed to worrying about such biblical verses. They seek to know what God expects of them, not what promises they might expect from God. The non-Jews, while accepting this explanation, still demanded an answer to their question. Rav Abbahu replied, "God punishes us little by little and so we can withstand the punishment; suffering is, therefore, a great blessing preventing our sins from overwhelming us." This answer satisfied the Christians and thus resolved the question originally posed. The existential problem of interfaith dialogue, however, remained, and the Gentiles inquired why Rav Abbahu could answer their question and Rav Safra could not. Rav Abbahu laughed and replied, "That's because I frequent your company."[6]

While the details of the story raise interesting questions of their own, the general framework provides a model for Jewish-Christian interaction. This story illuminates three aspects of that interaction. First, the conclusion of the tale suggests that Jewish self-understanding requires dialogue with others. Jewish exclusivism that refuses dialogue with non-Jews leads Jews to misunderstand their own tradition. Second, the content of the dialogue focuses on the Jewish claim to chosenness and the incongruity of that claim given the facts of Jewish history. Despite the inherent interest of the question of theodicy raised, the question of dialogical message seems more appropriate in this context: because non-Jews raise both the claim to chosenness and the details of Jewish history as important theological concerns, Jewish thinkers cannot avoid confronting them. A Jewish theology of Christianity must give full weight to the fact that Christians help shape the theological program Jews follow. Finally, the story begins by assuming an ecumenical world, a world in which Gentiles respect Jewish scholars and in which Jewish scholars respond to Gentile questions. A sharp-witted Jew could surely see behind the Gentile's query an attempt to undermine Jewish self-understanding; Rabbi Abbahu refused to let that hidden agenda deter him. So, too, the conversation between Jews and Christians cannot avoid a hint of conversionary zeal. No question ever arises from purely academic sources. Nevertheless, honest questions demand honest answers.

A Jew seeking theological understanding of a dialogue between Jew and Christian, then, must confront these three issues: the meaning of Christianity as an impetus for Jewish self-understanding, the Jewish need to heed the Christian agenda of Jewish theology, and the Jew's obligation to answer even those questions that apparently pre-judge the absurdity of Judaism. A Jew might well turn to the New Testament to find examples of how Christianity, not only in its origins but even today, challenges Jewish thinking. New Testament examples illustrate how questions raised by one type of Christian query of Judaism might stimulate a serious consideration of that query and point to a serious Jewish response to it. Irving Greenberg has called upon Jews and Christians to affirm the "fullness of the faith claims" of one another.[7] Jewish engagement with the New Testament promises to at least begin heeding that call.

DIALOGUE AS CONSTITUTIVE OF SELF-UNDERSTANDING

Some Jewish leaders, even in rabbinic times, displayed intellectual and personal courage by engaging in open dialogue with heretical thinkers. Despite a tendency to emphasize the importance of Judaism and the people of Israel, Rabbi Meir, the disciple of Rabbi Akiva in the second century, evinced a clear understanding of the essential necessity for dialogue with non-Jews and with Jewish heretics.[8] He cultivated friendship with philosophers such as Euonymous of Gadara and with Elisha Ben Abuya, known best as "Aher," the disciple who rejected tradition and became "other." Meir based his ecumenical perspective on a biblical precedent by a creative interpretation of Leviticus 18:5, "You shall therefore keep my statutes and my decrees, the doing of which keeps a person alive." The text, he noted, did not specify priests or Jews. God's laws apply to all human beings.[9] As Rabbi Meir reads the verse, God provides guidance suitable for humanity generally. Two implications follow from that conclusion: Torah laws apply to all people, not just to Jews, and Torah learning can be derived from any person, not merely from a Jew.

If the divine decrees apply to any person, then Jews must share them with others. Rabbi Meir's theology of divine law includes an impetus for reaching out to non-Jews. The precepts vouchsafed to Jews need dissemination to all humanity. Robert Gordis recognizes this aspect of Jewish tradition. He claims that while Jews may protect their unique identity by withdrawing from contact with non-Jews, they also lose their distinctive mission in the process. He declares: "Isolation would preserve the shell but not the spirit of the people that gave the Bible to mankind, whose prophets saw Israel as the Servant of the Lord proclaiming the basic religious and ethical truths to all men."[10] In that sense, Christians play an important role in Jewish theology as one audience with whom Jews share their knowledge of the divine will.

Rabbi Meir, however, probably understood his theology differently. If God's laws apply to all people, they can be explicated by looking at humanity generally, not merely at Jews. Conversation with non-Jews illuminates the meaning of the Jewish tradition itself. The midrash records that Rabbi Meir learned the meaning of Naomi's statement in Ruth 1:8, ". . . return each of you to her mother's house," from a non-Jewish philosopher, Euonymous. Rabbi Meir visited this philosopher to console him for the death of his mother and found the entire household in mourning. Then he visited again when the philosopher's father died, and discovered that this time no mourning took place. The philosopher replied using the proof text from Ruth to show that "for Gentiles the mother and not the father is most important."[11] Although the text from Ruth concerns Gentiles, Rabbi Meir could scarcely expect Euonymous to cite the passage. He learned more than just a new understanding of why the author of Ruth did not have Naomi tell her daughter-in-law to return to her father's home (as an Israelite daughter-in-law might). He also discovered that he could learn the meaning of the Torah from a non-Jew.

The rabbis looked upon certain Gentiles as sources of wisdom and inspiration, as expositors of the Torah. Rabbi Abba Ben Kahana, expressing this view, claimed that Balaam, in the time of Moses, and Euonymous, mentioned above, were the two greatest philosophers of the Gentiles. He gives as his example the story that the nations of the world repaired to Euonymous asking how they could cause Israel to assimilate —at least that is what I make out of the verb "l'hizdaveg," but other versions contend that the nations asked how they could attack Israel. Euonymous responded by telling them to look at Israel's schools. If children recite the prayers, then Israel cannot be assimilated since "the voice is the voice of Jacob and the hands are the hands of Esau"; thus "when Israel's voice is found in the synagogue, the nations cannot prevail; when its voice is not found there, the nations can prevail against them."[12] Euonymous apparently teaches the nations something about Israel's nature. More to the point, however, the rabbis learn from him the meaning of the text in Genesis 27:22. Here, as in the case of Rabbi Meir, the non-Jewish philosopher teaches the Jews how to interpret a biblical text. More importantly, Jews discover their own qualities, the basis of their particular talent, from this non-Jew.

Euonymous may not have intended evil toward the Jewish people. The text allows several interpretations. Other characters in the Bible and in rabbinic literature not only represent non-Jewish culture, but a hostile Gentile culture, the "enemy" who seeks to destroy Israel. The rabbis pair Euonymous, as noted earlier, with Balaam. Balaam's famous prophecy, "How goodly are your tents, O Jacob," in Numbers 24:5 takes on a similar meaning in rabbinic lore. According to the biblical story, Balak called Balaam to help him attack the Israelites and destroy them before they could conquer his land. Balaam speaks as an enemy of Israel, not merely as a non-Jew. According to the Bible, God prevented Balaam from fulfilling this wish, and so the prophet blessed the people instead of cursing them. The rabbis look at each of these blessings separately. Most of them, they contend, while literally blessings, did indeed become curses. Even a blessing when uttered with evil intentions takes on the power of a curse. The verse in Numbers 24, however, seems more like an exclamation than a blessing. Balaam seems astonished at Israel's "goodly tents." The rabbis explain this exclamation as a reference to Jewish schools. Balaam's approbation of Judaism, like that of Euonymous, confirms rabbinic views of the nature of Jewish religion: it is based on learning and study. This part of Balaam's prophecy, they report, did not turn into a curse. Balaam, like Euonymous, correctly appraises Jewish uniqueness: Israel's true strength lies in its spiritual power, in its educative force.[13] Another conclusion arising from this tale suggests the value Jews can find in the views of their enemies. Jews need Gentiles, even ones as hostile as Balaam, to teach them how to understand themselves, to learn the meaning of their own religious tradition.

When talmudic sources disguise anti-Christian polemic by assimilating them to the story of Balaam, the intention is far from laudable.[14] The attempt to mask criticism of one's enemy creates rancor within and without one's own community. The use of Balaam as an image of Israel's theological and political opponents, however, serves a positive function by suggesting how God sends critics against Jews to teach them more about themselves. From that perspective, Christianity precisely in its unflattering view of Judaism plays an essential role in Jewish self-understanding. Christians offer a critical voice by which Jews learn more about themselves. The very "curse" they offer turns into a blessing when, through it, Jews discover who they are and in what their peculiar virtues consist. The imperative to dialogue lies in the corrective value provided by an outside observer. Jews gain insight into their own destiny by attending to the theological agenda of others.

The various controversy stories in the New Testament did not arise as a means for helping Jews reach a better sense of self. Nevertheless, those stories illustrate how Christian criticism may lead to greater Jewish self-awareness. Looking at those tales, of course, one must take care not to elevate their message to an immutable truth. Jews, no less than Christians, need to heed Arland J. Hultgren's warning that "It is a vice, not a virtue, to continue to portray Judaism in the negative terms of these stories, even when it is so portrayed in these segments of the Scriptures of the Christian church."[15] The New Testament does not portray Jews realistically, even as they were in the time of Jesus, much less today. Nevertheless, the stories can stimulate Jewish self-reflection.

An open encounter with the polemic of Mark 7 suggests how Jews might find a place for Christian opposition in their own self-understanding. The chapter as a whole focuses on laws of purity and the difference between "Pharisaic" laws of purification, dedication of holy things, and dietary prescriptions with their attention to detail and Jesus' rejection of such amplification of biblical guidelines. Citing the well-known phrase from Isaiah 29:13 rejecting those who worship God with "doctrines created by mortals," Jesus reverses the requirements for purity: not what touches a person from the outside but what a person expresses from within determines that person's defilement (Mk 7:14–23). Judaism fails because it legitimates merely human laws as guidance for life. Christianity, the author of Mark suggests, succeeds because it realizes that God aims at transforming people, not merely behaviors.

Mark's theological purpose goes beyond this critique of religious behaviorism. As Howard Clark Kee remarks, the author of the passage seeks not merely to define "the purity of the covenant people" but also to produce "a redefinition of who the true covenant people are."[16] The text argues that those who focus exclusively on the forms of obedience misunderstand the meaning of obedience. The laws transform a person's life in order to transform the person's nature. The covenant people consists of those seeking self-transformation, not merely change in outward behavior. This definitional aspect of Mark 7 raises important questions for Jewish self-understanding. Those questions, however, should not distract from focusing on the behavioral issue. Jews, like all human beings, often become slaves of habit. Christian criticism may help release people from the shackles of unthinking custom.

Jewish thinkers often raise the same protest against religious behaviorism, often turning to the same texts that Mark 7 utilizes. Bachya Ibn Pakuda's devotional work *Duties of the Heart* refers to Isaiah 29:13 four times to criticize those who treat the commandments as merely concerned with external obedience.[17] Certain important differences between Mark and Bachya, however, separate the two. Bachya locates the problem in *how* Jews perform the commandments, not in the performance of the commandments themselves. If people think that external obedience fulfills their obligations, if they practice the commandments only out of fear of what others think of them, or if they have an incomplete trust in the divine, then, Bachya feels, they have impaired their religious life. When people fulfill the commandments out of love, in sincerity, and without hope of a reward, then the commandments do indeed lead to religious vitality. Secondly, Bachya emphasizes the inevitable weakness of human beings. Our eyes are clouded by ignorance and confusion; the evil impulse leads us astray; daily needs distract us. While Mark 7 decries those who fail to understand the importance of intention rather than mere obedience, Bachya sympathizes with them. Bachya agrees with Mark 7 that commandments observed only in external form lose their religious value. He disagrees with Mark's attempt to delegitimate those who fail to reach the highest goal.

Bachya's perception of the human condition provides a clue to the theological meaning Jews can find in Christian polemics. Human beings, because of their weakness and confusion, need an outsider to recall them to their ideals and higher aims. Jews who tend to fall into religious behaviorism may require just that challenge raised by Christians to remember the basic goal to which their behavior points. Martin Buber records that the holy Yehudi once summoned his disciple Simhah Bunam and instructed him to travel to a certain inn. Once there, Bunam and his companions set about preparing to stay. Since they would eat a meal at the inn, they concerned themselves with the preparation of the food. The tale relates that they "went in and out and asked all sorts of questions concerning the meat which was to be served them." A man dressed in rags watched them for some time with growing impatience. Finally, he scolded them, "O you hasidim," he said, "you make a big to-do about what you put into your mouths being clean, but you don't worry half as much about the purity of what comes out of your mouths." Rabbi Bunam was about to reply, but the wayfarer had already disappeared, for, the tale comments, this is Elijah's habit. Rabbi Bunam realized that he had heard the words meant for him and returned to the Yehudi, chastened and enlightened.[18] Insiders often fail to note their own lack of balance. They need to hear from others a reproof that recalls them to themselves.

Christianity speaks with such a voice reminding Jews of themselves and their obligations. Heeding that voice, Jews need not accept the Christian contention that being a covenant people depends upon an exalted fulfillment of the commandments. They need not regard the laws of their tradition as "precepts taught by men." Nevertheless, they do need to hear an outsider pointing out their excesses.

Jacob Bernard Agus has repeatedly called on Jews and Christians to recognize the necessity for mutual scrutiny. He recognizes in Judaism and Christianity two complementary pieties that check one another's excesses. Not only does he chart the various currents found within these two traditions, but he acknowledges the need for interaction between insiders and outsiders of any tradition. He declares that truth speaks with more than one voice: "It is only through the juxtaposition of several different points of view that any healing glimpse of truth may come to us."[19] God provides sources for these different viewpoints. In the case of Jews, dialogue with Christians enables us to hear complementary overtones necessary for a balanced life of faith. Naturally, many Jews react strongly when Christians question their sincerity and piety. All too often, however, the ignorance and confusion that Bachya considers the common human condition prevents us from questioning ourselves. God sends us a needed corrective to our blindness and unwillingness to probe our own intentions —the faithful accuser from the other side. Christians, when viewed from within the faith of Jewish belief, serve this role.

CHRISTIANS, JEWS, AND THE CHOSEN PEOPLE

As Howard Clark Kee noted, however, the thrust of the passage in Mark 7 goes beyond a corrective protest against religious behaviorism. It redefines the meaning of God's covenanted people, of the chosen community. The social and political challenge of Christianity to Jewish self-understanding has, historically, been even more pointed than the ritualistic or faith-oriented challenge. After Constantine established Christianity as a licit religion and then when, in his wake, Christianity emerged as the triumphant new religion of the west, Jews were forced to reconsider their role in the divine plan. The earliest Jewish responses to this challenge shaped the classic texts of Judaism as Jacob Neusner clearly shows. Neusner claims that both Jews and Christians in the fourth century needed to define themselves, for different reasons. Both used the biblical term "Israel" to solve their definitional problems. Jews interpreted those promises to Israel as the basis for hope in a better future; Christians used the same texts as premonition of their own experiences enabling them to ground their apparently "new" religion in an ancient tradition.[20]

Almost from their origins, then, Jews and Christians have debated the meaning of their legacy of the Hebrew Bible. They contend against one another for exclusive rights to the name of Israel. An important corollary to this struggle concerns their views of scriptures. Some modern thinkers understand the biblical tradition as a bridge linking Jews and Christians together. Robert Gordis, for example, claims that Jews and Christians share a common past, a past outlined and preserved in a "record of revelation enshrined in the same Sacred Scriptures, from Genesis to Chronicles."[21] Traditionally, however, Jews have been skeptical about that shared inheritance. Since from earliest times Christians appropriated the biblical legacy in ways that excluded Jewish claims, Jews reacted by denying the commonality.

Rabbi Judah, the son of Rabbi Shalom, explained how Jews could refute the contradictory biblical interpretations of Christian exegetes. He reported that Moses wanted to write the oral tradition as well as the written Torah. God, according to Rabbi Judah, realized that, once written, those texts could be translated. Once translated, non-Jews could claim the Torah as their own. God told Moses, Rabbi Judah claimed, that the nations would claim to be "the true Israel, the sons of God" and the Jewish counter-claim would appear to be equally valid. God would then test each claimant by demanding an explanation of "my mystery." That mystery, Rabbi Judah contends, is the Mishnah, the oral law. Without that mystery at hand, the meaning of the written law cannot be discerned. Without the Mishnah, the Christian claim to God's revelation proves false.[22] Merely sharing a content in common, merely sharing a set of texts, does not unite religious communities; the shared texts may cause dissension and debate.

A Jewish theology of Christianity must take that dissension over the meaning of the Bible seriously. God apparently desires that Jews dialogue with those who hold very different views of revealed truth. How should a Jew respond to a Christian interpreter of the biblical text? The apostle Paul in Galatians 3 uses Jewish midrashic exegesis against Jewish claims. He "presupposes a midrashic interpretation of the giving of the law which has much in common with contemporary exegetical traditions, but which Paul has turned against the law in a way characteristic of him."[23] The entire argument in Galatians 3 contends that God performs the miracle of salvation through spirit and hearing with faith rather than through legal prescriptions and their performance. The true heirs of Abraham consist of all who have faith, as Genesis 15:6 suggests and, according to Paul, as Habukkuk 2:4 confirms. Those true heirs include Jews and non-Jews, men and women, masters and slaves.

Paul's approach challenges Jewish self-understanding. Jews claim that as the chosen people, as a people with a special destiny, God provides them with a "great and extensive" tradition. The same verses that Paul uses to reject Jewish legalism offer believing Jews confirmation of their tradition. Jewish tradition affirms that the commandments govern and enhance the significance of every human activity. Through obedience to those laws people live better lives and serve God more fully. From this perspective, Paul's midrash on Genesis and Habakkuk appears disquieting. Hans Joachim Schoeps voices that disquiet when he charges that Paul suffers from a "fateful misunderstanding" that "tears asunder covenant and law."[24] This initial response to Paul arises from the depths of Jewish self-understanding. Nevertheless, Paul's criticism sets an agenda for Jewish theology. Covenant and commandment, self-evidently related as they seem, become problematic when exposed to Pauline criticism. Why should God assault Jews with the Pauline contradiction of covenantal promise and its implications?

Answering that question demands, first, looking at Paul's ideas in their own context, without the backlog of anti-Jewish sentiment that often accompanied them historically. When Christians used Paul's teaching to delegitimate Judaism, they not only transformed his intent but also obscured his meaning.[25] John Gager, following Lloyd Gaston, suggests that Paul directs his debate against Christian Judaizers, not against Jews. He rejected the claim that salvation comes exclusively through the practice of Jewish rituals. The focus of his attack, then, is not against the Jewish practice of Judaism, but against the Gentile practice of it. Paul urges that Jews narrow their focus; they have been chosen to follow one path to God; their destiny arises from its unique history; other peoples, however, discover different paths and need not exchange their destiny for that of the Jews. According to Gager, Paul argues that the Jewish covenant has no relevance for the Gentiles who must turn to another avenue for salvation. When Jews claim that their way represents an exclusive path to salvation, Paul must "disallow Israel's boasting as inappropriate." If he does not, then his mission to the Gentiles loses its meaning.[26] Galatians, on this reading, challenges Jews to reevaluate their relationship with non-Jews, to rethink the implications of their covenant identity for their interaction with the nations of the world. Paul suggests that Jews look at the nations with a more chastened attitude. The nations may have a justification and a legitimacy that Jews often ignore.

Jewish theology should include a cautionary attention to non-Jewish nations such as that which Paul expresses. Self-confidence won from covenantal identity may lead to a disparagement of those outside the covenant. Paul's polemic demands that Jews acknowledge the validity and righteousness of non-Jewish peoples. Jews should not reject the authority and legitimacy of Gentile nations merely because of their differences in religious belief. Jews must respect these nations as instruments of God no less than Israel itself. Traditional Jewish teachings parallel Paul's contention on this point. Rabbinic tradition enunciates a prohibition against Jewish rebellion against their state of exile. A striking example of the obligation to maintain respect for non-Jewish groups comes in relationship to the land of Israel. Jews have always looked yearningly homeward to that land and have never relinquished the hope of a restored Jewish state. Nevertheless, duties toward others, imposed by God, limit the means Jews can take in fulfilling their dream.

The Talmud tells that, at the time of the Jewish exile among the peoples, God caused Israel to swear two oaths: one required Jews to forswear using force to retake the land of Israel, the second prohibited rebellion against the nations of the earth.[27] This story suggests that God desires Jews to recognize the limits of political violence and of personal violence. Theologically, Christianity plays a divinely appointed role of reminding Jews of their oath to respect the rule of the nations, to grant the nations their own, unique, place in the divine scheme. Israel needs opponents to oppose the conceit of exclusivism with the alternative of co-existence.

God requires Jews to live up to their oath: they must respect the social and political sovereignty of non-Jews. Christianity's triumphalism tests Jewish loyalty to that oath in a peculiarly intense way. Respecting the Christian includes admitting the right of Christians to interpret the biblical texts according to their own readings without taking arms against a politically repressive ideology. Jews may disagree with those readings. Jews do disagree with one another on biblical interpretations. Disagreement does not entail disrespect. Bringing Christians into the arena of Jewish debate about biblical meanings embraces them as siblings in a family of related religions. Jewish and Christian debates on the "true Israel" appear as "controversies for the sake of heaven" and not merely political or social ideology. Sharing a universe of discourse within which Jews grant Christians their right to political sovereignty, in which biblical discussion does not become a surrogate for political in-fighting, changes the context of discussion. Jews and Christians now must attend to one another as equally authorized, equally authoritative articulators of the divine tradition.

Jews and Christians interact as siblings whose rivalry must give way now and again to family solidarity. Richard Rubenstein understands Paul's polemic against Judaism using this familial metaphor. He suggests that Paul often sounds extreme and antagonistic toward Jews precisely because he feels free to use "among the family" language he would not use outside of it. He suggests that "When Paul wrote that his fellow Jews had proven faithless to their God, he was speaking of his own kin in what he regarded as a family dispute. Things are often said within the family that have a very different meaning when repeated by outsiders."[28] A family shares a common history and past, but each member of the family experiences that commonality differently. One family member may hear another describe an event and complain that it didn't happen that way at all. Only when all the family members present their version of the tale can an outsider piece together the reality that unites them.

Through the same process Jews and Christians glean a comprehensive understanding of the Bible and its implications for their own self-understanding. Different views of scripture that separate Jews and Christians represent interpretations of a complex truth. The refractions of interpretation that each shares with the other provides a greater basis upon which to reconstruct the whole reality. The conclusion of the discussion why more of the Torah appears in oral tradition than in the written points to the essential need for such dialogue. Rabbi Judah ends by alluding to Hosea 8:12: "If I were to write for him the many things of my law they would be counted as strange." He suggests that the many things are the Mishnah which is larger than the law. Jews, he strikingly suggests, would find the Torah alien had they not shared in the process of expanding and developing it. Without the Mishnah, an oral tradition reflecting Jewish history and experience, the written law would appear strange, the product of an ancient and foreign culture. God, recognizing the problem, established its cure: for the sake of righteousness God multiplied Torah laws so as to glorify them.[29] When Jews reflect on the process of midrash, the means by which the alienated ancient text becomes meaningful in the present, they discover how their cultural distinctiveness has naturalized and domesticated the Bible.

Dialogue with non-Jews stimulates reflection on the meaning of midrash. As Jews participate with non-Jews in discussions about the Bible, they learn the essential role of their culture and history in naturalizing Torah law. Conversation with non-Jews, precisely on the meaning of Torah and its application, leads to an appreciation of how history shapes meaning. That realization teaches Jews that the Torah reflects culture, because it develops and grows with the historical life of the Jewish people. Through such dialogue Jews realize that they possess the Torah because of their cultural experience. Jews are chosen by the hand of historical destiny, not by a metaphysical quality of distinctiveness. Debate about the meaning of the Bible reminds all participants that God has as many "chosen" people as there are historically distinct communities.

THE HISTORY OF JUDAISM IN THE LIGHT OF CHRISTIANITY

The Jewish claim to represent the chosen Israel rests not only on the scriptural record, but also on a reading of the Jewish past. The Christian challenge to Jewish self-understanding, accordingly, includes a critique of both Jewish exegesis and the Jewish reading of history. One of the earliest such critiques appears in the book of Acts. Jews have indeed paid attention to that work and sought to decode its significance for them. Jacob

Agus studies the book and urges several "Jewish perspectives" on Christians seeking to understand that work: the work reflects a Jewish context, does not teach that Jews are rejected but that they will be in the eschatological future, that the issue dividing Jews from Christians is not universalism and particularism but rather the eschatological validity of the Torah, that the "Jews" opposed are "temple Jews," not later rabbinic Jews, that the events occur within the context of world history generally, and that the book seeks to overcome the isolation of Jews and thereby to eliminate, not perpetuate, antisemitism.[30] Agus' analysis suggests how Christians may move to dialogue even on the basis of such texts as the book of Acts which criticize Judaism. The present analysis, however, starts from another point of departure. How can a Jewish theology account for and take seriously the critique of Jewish history and historical claims advanced in the book of Acts. The question raised here asks not "What can Acts mean for Christians?" but rather "What can Acts mean for Jews?"

Taken in its totality, the book traces the transition from a Jewish Christianity centered in Jerusalem to a Gentile Christianity centered in Rome. Historians differ about the factual reliability of the book, but all agree that its central aim lies less in reporting facts than in providing a set of "typological" models for Christian self-understanding. One pervasive model focuses on the separation of Christianity from Judaism: "the Church came of age when it finally left Jerusalem behind."[31] Acts 7, Stephen's speech, provides a rationale for leaving Judaism behind. Until the final verses, nothing in the passage suggests that anyone other than a Jew composed it. The chapter reads much like Nehemiah 9 or Psalm 106, a review of Jewish history stressing the rebelliousness and contentiousness of the Jewish people.[32] Much of the chapter portrays Jewish heroes in a positive light. The covenant of circumcision, associated with Abraham in Acts 7, symbolizes Abraham's willingness to trust a promise for the future rather than demand immediate satisfaction. An extended description of Joseph shows how God raises up a hero to fulfill the divine promise. The story of Moses portrays Moses as a hero of the promise, equally wise and proficient in oratory (!) as any Hellenistic leader.

From the study of Moses onward the author emphasizes a single theme: Jewish misunderstandings of true leaders. The author incorporates Amos 5:25–27 to indicate how the early Israelites abandoned God, and the author even includes Solomon's temple in this critique, making a reference to Isaiah 66:1–2 to show that God, filling all heaven and earth, needs no temple (without, however, acknowledging that Solomon, according to 1 Kings 8:27–30, had already made the same point when dedicating the temple). The non-christological part of the passage culminates in a final charge: "You stiff-necked people, uncircumcised in heart and ears, you always resist the Holy Spirit" (Acts 7:51). Jews, in dialogue with Christians, need to heed that criticism and seek to understand its significance. The charge of recalcitrance, however, rankles. Do Jews need to read their history as a constant misunderstanding of the divine word? Why should God inflict such criticism on a people honoring the Torah?

The lessons of Jewish history sometimes leave behind painful memories. The history of biblical Israel and of early talmudic Judaism lies safely in a dimly recalled past transfigured by a holy literature. Even the persecutions of the middle ages are old wounds that, while retaining sensitivity, lack present urgency. The Nazi slaughter of six million Jews, however, remains an open wound, a continuing sore that causes immediate anguish. Under the impact of ecumenical dialogue, however, some modern theologians like Emil Fackenheim demonstrate the value of paying attention to the voice of God speaking from even our most recent history.[33] Conversation between Jew and non-Jew leads to productive insight concerning the meaning of historical disasters. Jews, looking critically at their own past, must examine assumptions about human nature, about God's role in history, and about relationships with non-Jews not usually scrutinized from within a Jewish standpoint. As Rabbi Abbahu suggested to his non-Jewish friends, Jews do not need to explain "evil" or disaster for themselves. They can accept the divine will as inscrutable but just. The need of non-Jews to know the meaning of such events, however, stimulates Jewish reflection on them. Moved by the needs of Gentiles who see God's hand working mysteriously in Jewish history, Jews themselves overcome an understandable reluctance and begin probing these painful memories. The Holocaust as a divine act does not challenge the fundamental assumptions of Jewish theology, but the disaster does suggest that Jews should reconceive the world within which they live. Jews need reminders of the continual need to reimagine reality.

Dialogue with non-Jews concerning the Nazi holocaust plays such a role. Some Jews like Richard Rubenstein focus their attention on how the lessons of the Holocaust undermine theology generally and suggest that the Nazis represent the ultimate fulfillment of modernization. Other Jews, recalled to the event by its importance in non-Jewish thinking, find in the questions raised by the Holocaust experience a valuable impetus to probing more deeply into how Jews and non-Jews interact, into their interdependency and common interests, and into the peculiarities that distinguish Jews from non-Jews. From the importance of the Holocaust as a human experience Jewish theologians learn to generalize from the specifics of Jewish history into broadly human principles. Christianity, then, by challenging Jews to confront the terrors of their history, fulfills an important role in recalling Jews to their general mission to humanity and awakening them from self-absorption. Reflection on the Holocaust stimulates a recognition that Jews and non-Jews alike face a secular society that challenges their basic assumptions about humanity and the world.

DISCOVERING A COMMON GROUND
FOR DIALOGUE IN OUR TIMES

Discussions about the Nazi holocaust reveal the one source of commonality binding Jews and Christians together, *nostra aetate,* "in our times." Religious people generally stand at a crossroads. While Jews and Christians do not share a single "tradition," they do meet at this "nexus," this intersection of secularity and religious values. While history and scripture fail to provide a link between Jews and Christians, the perils of our time do. Recognizing this truth, Arthur A. Cohen rejects the idea of a "Judeo-Christian tradition" because Jews and Christians disagree on most significant matters: faith, practice, view of divinity, and view of humanity. He admits, however, that a "Jewish-Christian nexus" has begun in modern times "born out of the crisis that threatens all humanity."[34] A Jewish theology of Christianity must make sense of that nexus, that meeting at the crossroads. How can Jews use the common confrontation with secularity to discover a connection with Christianity, a religion dedicated to the disconfirmation of Jewish faith?

Christian characterizations of Jewish religious life seem fixated on the negative and critical. The Christian scriptures themselves begin such characterizations. A peculiarly disturbing example occurs in the gospel of John, chapter 3, which portrays the rabbi Nicodemus as an insensitive and benighted model of Jewish religiousness. The text shows this representative of traditional Judaism as a hesitant disciple: he steals away at night to visit Jesus secretly, although convinced of Jesus' supernatural powers. When Jesus tells him that only one who has been reborn can see the kingdom of heaven, Nicodemus responds in an amazement that shows his lack of understanding. Jesus remarks, clearly astonished, "Are you a teacher of Israel and yet do not comprehend this?" By nature, it seems, official representatives of Judaism cannot grasp the significance of the Christ event.

Although this text judges Nicodemus rather harshly, later references to him seem positive. In the Sanhedrin, Nicodemus, at the risk of scorn, defends Jesus' right to a hearing (Jn 7:50–52). After the crucifixion he comes to anoint the body with a heavy load of spices (Jn 19:39). None of these instances retract the critique of chapter 3, but suggest that Nicodemus at least (and this essay focuses on precisely the Jewish perspective, that of Nicodemus) considered the encounter with Jesus a positive contribution to his religious life.

Many Jews cannot concur with Nicodemus' response. Martin Buber, certainly one Jew exceptionally open and receptive to the New Testament, felt constrained to reject this passage. Buber considered the gospel of John as a whole representative of Christianity's distortion of the basic Jewish intuition that truth grows out of interpersonal meeting, out of the responsive living of I-You exchange. He illustrated his concern by pointing to this conversation between Jesus and Nicodemus in John 3 as a primary example.[35] Buber claimed that the story took as its point of departure an historical reality: Jesus used the symbols of Jewish tradition, particularly those taken from the Genesis creation story, to advocate personal self-renewal. He called upon his audience to "follow me," and led them through his own example to a personal rebirth. Buber affirmed the Jewish value of this type of teaching: "By what he says Jesus does not intend to bar the way to heaven to his nocturnal visitor, but to open it." Buber lamented, however, that as the story evolved it came to mean the opposite of its original intention and eventually taught an exclusiveness of salvation. Jews, no matter how willing to heed the call of heaven, could not transcend their earthy nature. Only a person constituted of heavenly nature could understand the message that Jesus sent. Buber rejected that exclusivist doctrine.[36]

Buber's reading misunderstands the text and therefore misconstrues both the error attributed to Nicodemus and the appropriate response for a Jew when shown that error. As scholars have noted, the passage in John 3 reflects a general ascension myth prevalent in the Hellenistic period. Various Jewish pseudepigraphic narratives describe how ancient heroes ascended on high and returned with a secret doctrine. Recently, William C. Grese has commented that whereas traditional ascension stories offer manuals for a heavenly journey, "John 3 does not describe how to enter heaven for a revelation but how to obtain the revelation to be found in Jesus," a particularly significant variation on the traditional theme.[37]

Buber's own theory of human meeting should draw attention to the importance of this variation. Jesus says to Nicodemus that the road to the world to come lies not in a formula or manual of heavenly ascent. Instead, the earthly task must include finding a master whose life transmits the heavenly secrets and whose charisma brings a sense of rebirth. Buber recounts the story of Moshe Teitelbaum who dreamed that he had been in the paradise of the early rabbinic teachers (tannaim). There he saw the rabbis studying talmudic tractates and cried, "This can't be paradise." The angels corrected him, "You seem to think that the Tannaim are in paradise, but that's not so: paradise is in the Tannaim."[38] Buber himself considers the relationship between teacher and disciple the "quintessence" of Hasidic life. He considers the foundation of Hasidism to lie in "the life between those who quicken and those who are quickened." The truth of Hasidism, as Buber saw it, lay in discipleship rather than intellectual prowess, human ties with a human leader rather than a doctrine to be mastered, revival through life with another rather than revival as return to a philosophical proposition.[39]

The lesson Jesus taught Nicodemus (at least from a Jewish perspective) revolves around that truth. Christians teach Jews not to look for a mundane path or a leader whose guidance involves purely practical affairs. Instead Jews should seek the means to transcendence, a means that need not require literal ascent to a heavenly sphere but rather a metaphorical transfiguration. Grese points out that John 3 explicitly rejects the paradigm of a literal heavenly journey. Following Jesus as person achieves what the more literal ascension stories portray mythically. The message of John 3, given this interpretation, echoes some of Buber's own contentions: a mundane leader who inculcates practices for everyday living can point beyond that daily life to self-transcendence. One may assume that while Nicodemus did not become a disciple of Jesus, he nevertheless learned this lesson and respected Jesus for having taught it. Jews may differ from Christians on the question of exclusivity: God may well provide more than one path to self-transcendence. Being born again need not require "water and Spirit" (Jn 3:5) but rather "leather and wool" (i.e. the tefillin and prayer shawl of Jewish worship). The method of attaining transcendence may indeed separate Jew and Christian.

The search for common ground between Jew and Christian, *Nostra Aetate* begins with recognition of a generally religious yearning for transcendence. Christians remind Jews again and again that the purpose of everyday life lies beyond that life. Jewish mystics knew this truth; the Talmud understands it. Most Jews recognize the God-centered nature of their tradition when confronted with it. Nevertheless, the pressure of daily life itself often pushes this awareness away from consciousness. People often narrow their horizons to cope more easily with the challenges they face. Understandable as this practice is, people need reminders of their ultimate purpose, of a transcendent mission in their lives. When Jews and Christians meet in dialogue they each rediscover the transcendent task that underlies their mundane living.

Abraham Joshua Heschel already recognized this dimension of dialogue in his discussions with Vatican leaders prior to the issuing of *Nostra Aetate*. He saw that while on one level, that of specific practices, beliefs, and traditions, Jews and Christians differed, on another, deeper level, that of religious insight, of the foundations from which religions spring, they share common desire for transcendence. He sought to free dialogue from its concern with external differences to focus on the "depth theological" issues. Christians seemed to heed this call and understand his emphasis. Jews, however, often questioned Heschel's wisdom in cultivating such wide-ranging friendships. Heschel defended his viewpoint by noting the peculiar crisis of modern times. Today religions generally suffer from a lack of sensitivity to transcendence, a denial of its very possibility. The purpose of religion today, he suggested, must be to revive that deadened awareness of transcendent meaning. Heschel thus realized that religions "in our time" must meet at that nexus, that crossroad, where secularity challenges depth-theology. For Heschel:

> The supreme issue today is not the Halakhah for the Jew or the Church for the Christian, but the premise underlying both religions, namely, whether there is a pathos, a divine reality concerned with the destiny of man which mysteriously impinges upon history.[40]

Listening to the dialogue between Jesus and Nicodemus, Jews can learn the importance of that divine pathos, of searching to uncover the divine that impinges so mysteriously on history. That common search ultimately supports the other aspects of a Jewish theology of Christianity. From attention to the call to seek transcendence comes an awareness of the need for dialogue as a means of rethinking the meaning of Israel's past and future and of rediscovering self through interaction with others. Heeding Heschel's reminder, still relevant today, of the crucial importance of sensitivity to the divine stake in human actions, a Jewish theology of Christianity can discover the necessity of dialogue in our time as a divine impetus to religious living.

NOTES

1. See Eugene B. Borowitz, *Contemporary Christologies: A Jewish Response* (New York: Paulist Press, 1980), p. 34.

2. Edward Flannery, "Seminaries, Classrooms, Pulpits, Streets: Where We Have to Go," in *Unanswered Questions: Theological Views of Jewish-Catholic Relations*, edited by Roger Brooks (University of Notre Dame Press, 1988), p. 130.

3. See the discussion on these two points in Walter Jacob, *Christianity Through Jewish Eyes: The Quest for Common Ground* (Cincinnati: Hebrew Union College Press, 1974), pp. 236–37.

4. See Michael A. Singer, "Speculum Concilii: Through the Mirror Brightly," in *Unanswered Questions*, edited by Roger Brooks, pp. 105–27; cited passages are on pp. 116 and 109.

5. *Genesis Rabba* 78:14. On Rav Abbahu's relationship with Christians and Christianity generally, see R. Travers Herford, *Christianity in Talmud and Midrash* (Clifton: Reference Books Publishers, 1966, reprint of 1903 edition), pp. 266–78.

6. *Avodah Zarah* 4a; Herford contends that the Gentiles "mentioned here were Jewish Christians, and of a strongly Jewish type . . ."; he also omits Abbahu's explanation of why he rather than Rav Safra can respond to the question (Herford, *Christianity in Talmud and Midrash*, p. 270).

7. See Irving Greenberg, "The Relationship of Judaism and Christianity: Toward a New Organic Model," in *Twenty Years of Jewish-Catholic Relations*, edited by Eugene J. Fisher, A. James Rudin, and Marc H. Tanenbaum (New York: Paulist Press, 1986), pp. 191–211.

8. Certainly one would not gain such a positive view of Meir's relationship to non-Jews from Herford, *Christianity in Talmud and Midrash*, since the various quotations in that work interpret him as anti-Christian (a careful reading of the various texts might lead to a more sympathetic interpretation). The characterization given here follows that of Graetz who notes that "He obtained his deep knowledge of men by mixing with those against whom prejudice prevailed" (Heinrich Graetz, *History of the Jews* Volume 2. Philadelphia: Jewish Publication Society of America, 1893, p. 437; see the entire biographical sketch given on pp. 435–40).

9. *Sifra* on Leviticus 18:5.

10. Robert Gordis, *Judaism in a Christian World* (New York: McGraw-Hill, 1966), p. xxvii.

11. *Ruth Rabba* 2:14.

12. *Genesis Rabba* 65:20.

13. *T. B. Sanhedrin* 105b.

14. See the discussion in Herford, *Christianity in Talmud and Midrash*, pp. 64–78.

15. Arland J. Hultgren, *Jesus and His Adversaries: The Form and Function of the Conflict Stories in the Synoptic Traditions* (Minneapolis: Augsburg, 1979), p. 200.

16. Howard Clark Kee, *Community of the New Life: Studies in Mark's Gospel* (Philadelphia: Westminster Press, 1977), p. 149.

17. See Bachya Ibn Pakuda, *Duties of the Heart,* English translation by Moses Hyamson (Jerusalem: Feldheim, 1970), Volume I, pp. 227, 307; Volume II, pp. 147, 233.

18. Martin Buber, *Tales of the Hasidim: The Later Masters,* translated by Olga Marx (New York: Schocken, 1961), p. 229.

19. Jacob Bernard Agus, *Dialogue and Tradition: The Challenges of Contemporary Judeo-Christian Thought* (New York: Abelard-Schuman, 1971), p. x.

20. Neusner discusses this point in several places; see, for example, Jacob Neusner, "Who Is Israel? The Jewish-Christian Confrontation in Fourth Century Iran," in *New Perspectives on Ancient Judaism, Volume 2, Religion, Literature and Society in Ancient Israel, Formative Christianity and Judaism: Ancient Israel and Christianity* (Lanham: University Press of America, 1987), pp. 151–72; *Understanding Seeking Faith: Essays on the Case of Judaism, Volume II: Literature, Religion, and the Social Study of Judaism.* Brown Judaica Studies 73 (Atlanta: Scholars Press, 1986), 119–42.

21. Robert Gordis, *The Root and the Branch: Judaism and the Free Society* (Chicago: University of Chicago Press, 1962), p. 1.

22. *Pesikta Rabbati* 14b.

23. Terrance Callan, "Pauline Midrash: The Exegetical Background of Gal 13:19b," *Journal of Biblical Literature* 99 (1980), p. 564; see also the discussion by Sam K. Williams, "*Promise* in Galatians: A Reading of Paul's Reading of Scripture," *Journal of Biblical Literature* 107 (1988), 709–20.

24. Hans Joachim Schoeps, *Paul: The Theology of the Apostle in the Light of Jewish Religious History,* translated by Harold Knight (Philadelphia: Westminster, 1961), p. 218; see the entire discussion on "Paul's Teaching About the Law," and his focus on the Galatians passage, pp. 168–218.

25. See Stanley K. Stowers, "Text as Interpretation: Paul and Ancient Readings of Paul," in *New Perspectives on Ancient Judaism Volume 3: Judaic and Christian Interpretation of Texts: Contents and Contexts* (Lanham: University Press of America, 1987), pp. 17–27.

26. See John B. Gager, *The Origins of Anti-Semitism: Attitudes Toward Judaism in Pagan and Christian Antiquity* (New York: Oxford University Press, 1985), "Paul's Discussion of Israel," pp. 230–46; "What Was the Heart of Paul's Argument with Jews, His Kinsmen by Race," 247–64.

27. *T. B. Ketubot* 111a.

28. Richard L. Rubenstein, *My Brother Paul* (New York: Harper and Row, 1972), p. 115.

29. *Bamidbar Rabba* Nasah 14:10.

30. See Jacob Bernard Agus, "Perspectives for the Study of the Books of Acts," in his *The Jewish Quest: Essays on Basic Concepts of Jewish Theology* (New York: Ktav, 1983), pp. 239–48.

31. J.C. O'Neill, *The Theology of Acts in Its Historical Setting* (London: SPCK, 1961), p. 71. On the meaning and importance of the book of Acts generally, see the entire issue of *Interpretation* 42 (1988); Martin Hengel, *Acts and the*

History of Earliest Christianity (Philadelphia: Fortress, 1980); Henry J. Cadbury, *The Book of Acts in History* (London: Adam and Charles Black, 1955); Martin Dibelius, *Studies in the Acts of the Apostles* (London: SCM Press, 1956).

32. On Stephen's speech see O'Neill, *Theology of Acts,* pp. 71–89 and Earl Richard, "The Polemical Character of the Joseph Episode in Acts 7," *Journal of Biblical Literature* 98:2 (1979):255–67.

33. See Emil L. Fackenheim, *To Mend the World: Foundations of Future Jewish Thought* (New York: Schocken, 1982).

34. Arthur A. Cohen, *The Myth of the Judeo-Christian Tradition* (New York: Harper and Row, 1970), p. xx.

35. Martin Buber, *Two Types of Faith,* translated by Norman P. Goldhawk (New York: Macmillan, 1952), pp. 117–26.

36. Ibid. pp. 124–25.

37. William C. Grese, "Unless One Is Born Again: The Use of a Heavenly Journey in John 3," *Journal of Biblical Literature* 107 (1988), pp. 677–93.

38. Buber, *Tales of the Hasidim: The Later Masters,* pp. 189–90.

39. Martin Buber, *Tales of the Hasidim: The Early Masters,* translated by Olga Marx (New York: Schocken, 1961), p. 8.

40. Abraham Joshua Heschel, "From Mission to Dialogue," *Conservative Judaism* 21:3 (1967), p. 2.

Jewish Theologian and Christian Apologist: Will Herberg on Judaism and Christianity

David G. Dalin

FROM MARXISM TO JUDAISM: THE RELIGIOUS EVOLUTION OF A JEWISH THEOLOGIAN

When Will Herberg died in March of 1977, American Judaism lost one of its most provocative religious thinkers of the post-World War II generation. Like Hermann Cohen and Franz Rosenzweig before him, Herberg came to Judaism from the outside. A Marxist and atheist through much of his young adulthood, Herberg had received no Jewish education or religious training in his youth, and he turned to the study of Judaism and Christianity only after his romance with Marxism ended. A prolific and influential Jewish theologian and Jewish interpreter of Christian religious thought, beginning in the late 1940s, his spiritual journey from Marxism to Judaism and the Jewish understanding of Christianity was unique in the American Jewish intellectual history of this century. The only Jewish ex-Marxist to embrace Jewish theology and the study of religion as a full-time vocation, Will Herberg was the quintessential "baal teshuvah" of his generation.

Herberg was born in the Russian village of Liachovitzi in 1901. His father, Hyman Louis Herberg, who had been born in the same Russian *shtetl,* moved his family to the United States in 1904. When his family arrived in America, his parents, whom he would later describe as "passionate atheists," were already committed to the faith that socialism would bring salvation to mankind and freedom from the restraints that had bound western societies for centuries. His father died when Herberg was ten and his mother shared her husband's "contempt" for the Ameri-

143

can public school system. Although he attended Public School No. 72 in Brooklyn and Boys' High School, Herberg was largely self-taught, his real education taking place at the kitchen table of an apartment on Georgia Avenue in a lower-middle-class neighborhood of Brooklyn. A precocious and versatile student from his early youth, Herberg had learned Greek, Latin, French, German and Russian by the time he was a teenager. Graduating from Boys' High School in 1918, Herberg later attended CCNY and Columbia University, where he studied philosophy and history, without apparently ever completing the course work for an academic degree.

Herberg inherited his parents' "passionate atheism" and equally passionate commitment to the socialist faith. A regular contributor to communist journals such as the *Workers Monthly* during the 1920s and early 1930s, Herberg was also a familiar ideologue and polemicist in the *Modern Quarterly,* one of the chief theoretical journals of the Old Left generation.

As the 1930s progressed, however, Herberg became more and more disenchanted with his earlier Marxist faith. The grotesque Stalinist purges, the communist "betrayal" of the Popular Front on the battlefields of Spain during the Spanish Civil War, the Russian invasion of Finland and the Stalin-Hitler Non-Aggression Pact of 1939 all contributed to his growing disillusionment. His final break with orthodox Marxism, which came in 1939, was no mere change in political loyalties, no mere repudiation of the political radicalism of his youth. For, as he would confess in recounting his journey from Marxism to Judaism on the pages of *Commentary* in January 1947, Marxism had been, to him and to others like him, "a religion, an ethic and a theology; a vast all-embracing doctrine of man and the universe, a passionate faith endowing life with meaning."[1]

Put to the test, however, this Marxist faith had failed. Reality, as Herberg would later express it, "could not be forever withstood," and by the late 1930s he had begun to recognize that the all-encompassing system of Marxist thought could not sustain the values that had first attracted him to revolutionary activity. "Not that I felt myself any the less firmly committed to the great ideals of freedom and social justice," he would reflect in 1947. Rather:

> My discovery was that I could no longer find basis and support for these ideals in the materialistic religion of Marxism. . . . This religion itself, it now became clear to me, was in part illusion, and in part idolatry; in part a delusive utopianism promising heaven on earth in our time, and in part a totalitarian worship of collective man; in part a naive faith in the finality of economics, material production; in part a sentimental

optimism as to the goodness of human nature, and in part a hard-boiled amoral cult of power at any price. There could be no question to my mind that as religion, Marxism had proved itself bankrupt.[2]

Perceiving Marxism as a "god that failed," rather than as a "mere strategy of political action," Herberg was left with an inner spiritual void, "deprived of the commitment and understanding that alone made life livable."

As the god of Marxism was thus failing him in the late 1930s, Herberg chanced to read Reinhold Niebuhr's *Moral Man and Immoral Society*, a book that was to profoundly change the course of his life. "Humanly speaking," he would later write, "it converted me, for in some manner I cannot describe, I felt my whole being, and not merely my thinking, shifted to a new center. . . . What impressed me most profoundly was the paradoxical combination of realism and radicalism that Niebuhr's 'prophetic' faith made possible. . . . Here was a faith that warned against all premature securities, yet called to responsible action. Here, in short, was a 'social idealism' without illusions, in comparison with which even the most 'advanced' Marxism appeared confused, inconsistent, and hopelessly illusion-ridden."[3] More than any other American thinker of the 1930s and 1940s, Niebuhr related theology to politics through a realistic assessment of human nature that seemed inescapably relevant in a time of the breakdown of the Marxist (and liberal) faith in progress and human enlightenment. In the writings of Reinhold Niebuhr, Herberg discovered a compelling theological realism from which to derive and affirm his own post-Marxist religious and political faith.

Some of Herberg's acquaintances would later liken his rejection of communism, and return to Judaism, to Paul's conversion on the road to Damascus. The comparison may have pleased him, for Herberg always felt that his return to Judaism was similarly the product of events equally unanticipated and dramatic. His memorable road to *teshuvah,* inspired by his first encounter with Niebuhr, was unique in the annals of American Jewish intellectuals of the past generation. In an autobiographical passage of one of his essays, Herberg said that his encounter with Niebuhr's thought in 1939 was the "turning point," even before he personally met Niebuhr, who was then teaching at Manhattan's Union Theological Seminary. Like Franz Rosenzweig before him, whose writings he began to read during the early 1940s, Herberg went through a wrenching inner struggle over whether to become a Christian. After several soul-searching meetings with Niebuhr, Herberg declared his intention to embrace Christianity. Niebuhr counseled him, instead, to first explore his Jewish religious tradition and directed him across the street to the Jewish Theological Seminary, where Herberg went to study. The professors and students at the seminary undertook to instruct Herberg in Hebrew and Jewish thought.

Throughout much of the 1940s, while he was earning a living as the educational director and research analyst of the International Ladies Garment Workers Union, Herberg also devoted much of his time and energy to the study of Jewish sources. Not having received a traditional Jewish education in his youth, Herberg was introduced to the classical sources of Judaism through the writings of Solomon Schechter and George Foot Moore, and through the instruction of Judaic scholars who became his friends, such as Professors Gerson D. Cohen and Seymour Siegel, and the late Rabbi Milton Steinberg. As Seymour Siegel has reminisced, Herberg was "extraordinarily moved" by the realistic appraisal of human nature in the rabbinic literature, especially as expounded by Schechter.[4] He was also impressed by the theological writings of Martin Buber and Franz Rosenzweig who, together with Niebuhr, would shape his evolving views on religious existentialism and biblical faith.

Herberg was inspired and excited by what he learned. In Judaism he found, after years of searching, a faith that encouraged social action without falling into the trap of utopianism. Throughout the 1940s he met regularly with rabbis and students at the seminary, developing and explicating his emerging theology of Judaism. At the same time he began to write on Jewish theology for journals such as *Commentary* and the *Jewish Frontier,* and he began lecturing, on religious faith and the social philosophy of Judaism, to synagogue groups and on college campuses. In much demand as a speaker, he traveled widely, and gained the reputation of being "the Reinhold Niebuhr of Judaism." He met regularly, moreover, at his home with rabbinical students, and others, to discuss his theological ideas. In those early days, as one of these students has remembered, "when the naturalistic theology so brilliantly expounded by Professor Mordecai Kaplan was the main intellectual influence in Jewish religious circles, we were fascinated by Herberg's espousal of the orthodox ideas of a supernatural God, Messiah and Torah, expounded with fervor and yet interpreted in a new way."[5]

MORE CHRISTIAN THAN JEWISH?
THE THEOLOGY OF JUDAISM AND MODERN MAN

Out of these intellectual encounters, and out of several essays published in *Commentary* and elsewhere in the late 1940s, came Herberg's first major work, *Judaism and Modern Man,* which appeared in 1951. Widely acclaimed as a carefully reasoned and intensely written interpretation of Judaism in the light of the newest existentialist thinking, *Judaism and Modern Man* was highly praised by Jewish scholars, while Niebuhr himself believed that the book "may well become a milestone in the religious thought of America."

Herberg's central theological concern, as he describes it in *Judaism and Modern Man,* is the plight of modern secular man, his spiritual frustration and despair. One by one, Herberg examines the various "substitute faiths" in which modern man has placed his hopes and aspirations—Marxism, liberalism, rationalism, science, and psychoanalysis, among others—and finds that each is a way of evading ultimate theological issues. As a religion, as a basis of faith, each of these secular ideologies is found wanting. Modern man, claims Herberg, requires belief in an absolute God. "Man must worship something," Herberg often wrote. "If he does not worship God, he will worship an idol made of wood, or of gold, or of ideas."[6] Faith in God, asserts Herberg, is essential to one's being. Moreover, intellectual affirmation is not enough. A "leap of faith" is called for, a return to the living God of Abraham, Isaac and Jacob and a total commitment to him.[7]

In presenting his view of God and Judaism, Herberg criticized those theologians of the late 1930s and 1940s who espoused a liberal, rational approach to God and, in so doing, reduced God to an idea.[8] For the religious existentialist, such as Herberg, who was deeply influenced by the dialogical I-Thou philosophy of Buber and Rosenzweig, the "idea of God" is meaningless: God is important only if there is a personal relationship to him. Thus, for Herberg, Jewish faith and theology cannot be predicated upon an abstract idea of God such as, for example, the reconstructionist notion of "a power that makes for salvation." Rather, the God of *Judaism and Modern Man* is a personal God to whom we can pray with an expectation of a response,[9] with whom we can enter into a genuine dialogue.

In many respects, as Seymour Siegel has noted, Herberg's theology was quite traditional. He believed in revelation, covenant, the resurrection of the dead, and the coming of the messiah.[10] He also affirmed, unequivocally, the traditional theological doctrine of "chosenness." Jewish existence, argued Herberg, "is intrinsically religious and God oriented. Jews may be led to deny, repudiate and reject their 'chosenness' and its responsibilities, but their own Jewishness rises to confront them as refutation and condemnation."[11] At the same time, however, Herberg was not a fundamentalist: That is, he did not view scripture and the tradition as literally God's word. Thus, for example, while believing in revelation, Herberg did not accept "the Fundamentalist conception of revelation as the supernatural communication of information through a body of writings which are immune from error because they are quite literally the writings of God . . . the Bible is obviously not simply a transcript from His dictation."[12] Rather, Herberg regarded revelation as "the self-disclosure of God in His dealings with the world,"[13] through his active intervention in history, and the torah as a "humanly mediated record of revelation." In this, and in other respects, his theology, while traditional, was at variance with Orthodoxy.

Herberg argued, moreover, that a Jewish theology relevant to the post-war period would have to be predicated upon a less optimistic image of man, upon a sober recognition of human sinfulness and human limitations. The barbarities of Stalinism and, especially, the Nazi holocaust seemed to Herberg to have destroyed the very foundations of the prevailing liberal faith, shared by Reform and Reconstructionist Judaism alike, in the "natural goodness" of man. Liberal Jewish theology, he maintained, failed to answer the critical question of how evil regimes and institutions could possibly have arisen if man is essentially good. The answer, Herberg wrote, could be found in "Niebuhr's rediscovery of the classical doctrine of 'original sin,' which religious liberalism and secular idealism combined to deride and obscure." Sin, Herberg wrote, "is one of the great facts of human life. It lies at the root of man's existentialist plight." Without an "understanding of the nature of sin," he concluded, "there is no understanding of human life . . . or man's relation to God."[14]

Herberg's existentialist approach to Jewish theology struck a responsive chord in the hearts of many within the Jewish community and beyond who were searching for religious roots and spiritual inspiration. The publication of *Judaism and Modern Man* was greeted with praise and enthusiasm by several respected Jewish reviewers, such as Milton Konvitz and Rabbi Milton Steinberg. Indeed, in a pre-publication review, Steinberg went so far as to say that Herberg "had written the book of the generation on the Jewish religion." Some, in the Jewish community, however, found his approach to Jewish theology disturbing.

Especially disturbing for traditional Jews was the fact that his theology seemed to be more Christian than Jewish. Many of Herberg's Jewish readers complained that he was too pessimistic about human nature, that the doctrine of original sin invoked by Niebuhr was a theological category neither inherent nor central to Judaism. To be sure, neither Herberg nor even Niebuhr posited man's "complete usefulness." Nevertheless, as critics of Herberg have duly noted, the difference between their emphasis and that of traditional Judaism is unmistakable, even though one may discover, as Herberg does, passages from the Talmud that in isolation convey the impression of a sin-preoccupied culture. Time and again, Herberg's critics have pointed out how much else of his theology derives from Protestant theological sources and categories.[15] The influence of Christian theology, as S. Daniel Breslauer has suggested, is evident when Herberg calls for "an ethic of perfection," and one is reminded of the Christian exaltation of "an impossible ethics."[16] The influence of Christian theological thinking is also apparent in Herberg's discussion of the concept of salvation: "Salvation," wrote Herberg, "is salvation from sin because it is sin . . . which alienates us from God, disrupts society and brings chaos to the world . . . salvation is by faith and grace alone. . . . From the pit of sin we can be saved only by God's grace."[17] As Robert Gordis has correctly noted, however, the very concept of "salvation" is alien to traditional Jewish religious thought: "The idea of salvation . . . is, to be sure, central to Christianity. It is, however, so far from basic to Judaism that no Hebrew term for the concept exists in the vast expanses of Jewish religious literature, from the Bible through the Talmud and Midrash to the medieval philosophers, and even modern writers have yet to find an adequate Hebrew term for the idea."[18]

In formulating his new, existentialist theology of Judaism, Herberg borrowed the thought and terminology of Protestant thinkers, such as Niebuhr and Tillich, which were as incongruent with Judaism as they were congruent with Christianity.[19] As a result, *Judaism and Modern Man,* in retrospect, seems to be an assessment of Judaism from a Protestant rather than from a Jewish viewpoint. As such, during the past two decades, it has had little to say to a new generation of Jewish theologians and laity, for whom a Christian existentialist approach to Jewish faith is no longer relevant.

Herberg's most famous book, unquestionably, is *Protestant–Catholic–Jew,* which was published in 1955, and which remains a work of enduring value to anyone hoping to understand the sociology of American religion. It has become a classic work in American religious sociology, one that Nathan Glazer has called "the most satisfying explanation we have been given as to just what is happening to religion in America." The critical and public acclaim that greeted the publication of *Judaism and Modern Man* and, especially, *Protestant–Catholic–Jew* brought Herberg the academic recognition, and position, he had long sought. In 1955 he was offered a full-time academic appointment as professor of Judaic Studies and Social Philosophy at Drew University, a Methodist institution in New Jersey, where he would teach until his retirement in 1976, the year before his death. Herberg was the first American Jewish theologian to receive a full-time academic appointment, as a professor of Judaic studies, at a Christian denominational university in America.

During the 1950s and 1960s, while teaching at Drew, Herberg lectured at numerous universities and Christian seminaries, and was invited to speak from the pulpits of churches and synagogues throughout the United States and Europe. He published scholarly anthologies of the writings of Martin Buber, Karl Barth, Jacques Maritain, Paul Tillich and other modern existentialist theologians, and wrote several important essays dealing with the relationship between Judaism and Christianity, biblical theology and various aspects of Christian religious thought. As his friend and colleague, Bernhard W. Anderson, dean of the Drew Theological School, would later note, Herberg had a profound and enduring influence "upon his colleagues and upon generations of students, many of whom were training for the Christian Ministry."[20] As a committed Jew and as a Jewish theologian writing and speaking about Christianity during the 1950s and 1960s, moreover, Herberg had an influence on the Christian community that "extended far beyond his home university."[21] As a Jewish theologian of Christianity, who spoke often at Christian forums, Herberg insightfully interpreted and defended Christianity and, in so doing, helped Christians to reach a deeper understanding of their own religious faith. Indeed, his essays on Christian thought exhibit a sympathetic understanding and appreciation of Jesus and Christianity matched by few Jewish theologians of his generation.

HERBERG ON JESUS AND CHRISTIANITY

Herberg's writings were especially notable for their portrayal of Jesus in a way that showed "a deep appreciation for his ultimate significance to Christianity."[22] Herberg was not, of course, the first twentieth century Jewish thinker to write about Jesus in a sympathetic light. While some earlier Jewish scholars had been reticent to write sympathetically about the personality and teachings of Jesus because of the fact that Jews had been "so severely persecuted by Christians in the name of Jesus,"[23] several late nineteenth and early twentieth century European Jewish and American Jewish thinkers endeavored to establish a better intellectual understanding between liberal Christians and Jews through the study of the common ideological background of ancient Judaism and early Christianity, as revealed in parallels between rabbinic literature and the gospels, and the analysis of the Jewish sources and background of Jesus' moral and ethical teachings. In so doing, they had sought to develop a distinctively Jewish approach to, and understanding of, the life and teachings of "the historic Jesus," and to justify its relevance for Judaism.[24] Reflecting this new Jewish view, Professor Morris Jastrow of the University of Pennsylvania could write in 1899 that "from the historic point of view, Jesus is to be regarded as a direct successor of the Hebrew prophets," while the American Jewish communal leader Jacob Schiff could state that "we Jews honor and revere Jesus of Nazareth as we do our own prophets who preceded him."[25] When, in 1925, the distinguished Philo scholar and Jewish authority on the church fathers, Harry A. Wolfson of Harvard University, wrote an introductory essay to Joseph Jacobs' book *Jesus as Others Saw Him,* entitled "How the Jews Will Reclaim Jesus," Wolfson argued that Jews would reclaim Jesus as one of their own rabbis whose parables and sermons have a rightful place in Jewish literature alongside those of other ancient sages.[26] By the time of Wolfson's essay, a growing number of Jewish scholars and theologians, including Claude G. Montefiore, Leo Baeck, Joseph Klausner and Stephen S. Wise among others, had similarly begun to "reclaim" Jesus as a great prophet, moral teacher and/or rabbi within the normative Jewish tradition.[27]

Although the "Jewish reclamation" of Jesus was thus already well under way during the 1920s, the subsequent writings of Jewish theologians such as Martin Buber and Herberg contributed immeasurably to this enterprise. In an oft-quoted passages in *Two Types of Faith,* Buber, who profoundly influenced Herberg's understanding of Jesus and Christianity, and whom Herberg frequently cited, had written: "From my youth onwards, I have found in Jesus my great brother. That Christianity has regarded and does regard him as God and Saviour has always appeared to me a fact of the highest importance which, for his sake and my own, I must endeavor to understand. . . . My own fraternally open relationship to him has grown ever stronger and clearer, and today [in 1950] I see him more strongly and clearly than ever before. I am more than ever certain that a great place belongs to him in Israel's history of faith and that this place cannot be described by any of the usual categories."[28] This is a personal view of Jesus that Herberg implicitly shared and understood. Like Buber, Herberg found nothing alien in the teachings of Jesus, and he considered them to be almost entirely within the realm of Judaism. In his essay "A Jew Looks at Jesus," Herberg affirmed Jesus as a "great and incomparable moral teacher . . . [whose] exhortations and discourses stand unrivaled in . . . ethical literature. . . . By the common testimony of mankind, this Jewish rabbi from Nazareth . . . reached the high-water mark of moral vision of ethical teaching."[29] Following "entirely in the line of rabbinical tradition," Jesus' moral teachings, argued Herberg, "have their sources and parallels in the contemporary religious literature of the Jews from whom he sprang and among whom he taught. . . . As a moral teacher, he is a Jewish rabbi of great power and insight, drawing upon the traditional wisdom of his people."[30] Following Buber, however, Herberg believed that the faith of Jesus was akin to the faith of Amos and Isaiah, and that Jesus, being more than just a great moral teacher, carried on the prophetic legacy of ancient Israel:

> If the prophet is the God possessed man standing over against the community to which he belongs, bringing to bear upon it the word of the Lord in judgement and promise, then Jesus of Nazareth was a prophet of Israel, in the succession of Amos, Hosea, Isaiah and Jeremiah. His denunciations of the corruptions and idolatries of the age, his call to repentance, his promise of divine grace for those of a broken heart and a contrite spirit, his proclamation of the new age to come as judgement and fulfillment, follows . . . the pattern of the great prophets. . . . Jesus, the rabbinic teacher, is also among the prophets of Israel, with clear affinities to the great prophets of the past.[31]

Such a Jewish understanding of Jesus as prophet and moral teacher, maintained Herberg, offered no theological dilemmas for believing Jews, who could and should "reclaim" Jesus for Judaism, emphasizing the Jewish elements of his sayings and, especially, his continuity of the prophetic tradition: "Jesus' prophetic proclamations follow the prophetic word of his predecessors; his denunciations of the self-righteous 'scribes and Pharisees' can be abundantly paralleled in the literature of rabbinic self-criticism; the promise he held out of divine mercy for the repentant sinner was a promise which every contemporary Jew could understand even if he could not prevail upon himself to take hold of it."[32]

Like Buber and Franz Rosenzweig before him, Herberg recognized the reality of Christianity as a path to God. Herberg's insight into, and theological understanding of, the relationship between Judaism and Christianity was especially influenced by the writing of Rosenzweig, another twentieth century Jew who almost became a Christian until he was led, as he so aptly put it, "to return to where I have been elected from birth."[33] Indeed, in his seminal 1950 essay on Rosenzweig, which remains today one of the most perceptive brief introductions to Rosenzweig's thought, Herberg noted that "one of Rosenzweig's most profound and significant insights is his conception of the nature of Christianity and its relation to Judaism."[34] Understanding Christianity, as did Rosenzweig, as "Judaism for the Gentiles," through which the peoples of the world are brought to the God of Israel, Herberg viewed Judaism and Christianity as compatible theologies, being "virtually identical in their structure of faith."[35] For Herberg, as for Rosenzweig, the underlying unity of Christianity and Judaism had as its basis the "double covenant" theory, originally formulated by Rosenzweig during the 1920s, according to which God had entered into one covenant with the Jews and another with the Gentiles, through which they enter into an equally valid relationship with the divine. "Christian faith," argued Herberg, "brings into being and defines a new covenant, which is new not in the sense of supplanting the old but in the sense of extending and enlarging it, very much as we speak of the New World side by side with the Old. . . ."[36] Thus, for Herberg, the first covenant—the covenant with Israel—was extended and enlarged to "include the people of the Christian Church. . . . Instead of one community superseding the other, there are now two communities that are to work together for the sake of the one God with whom each has a viable covenantal relationship."[37] And the vocation of Christianity is thus to bring the nations of the world into the covenant. "Israel," said Rosenzweig (in a passage quoted by Herberg in his essay on Jesus), "can bring the world to God only through Christianity."[38] As a result, Herberg recognized that both faiths shared much in common, including a belief in the biblical God of Abraham, Isaac and Jacob, the understanding that the covenant established with Abraham signified the break with paganism and the advent of an "authentic relation with God," and a shared view of revelation and of scripture as being "in some sense both vehicle and record of such revelation."[39]

Herberg's understanding of the interrelationship between Christianity and Judaism, however, diverged from that of Rosenzweig's in one highly significant way: Herberg proposed that both are fundamentally historical religions, in which the history of faith is viewed from the perspective of "Heilsgeschichte," or redemptive history, according to which a single event is the instrument of redemption. Thus Christianity and Judaism, maintained Herberg, "are historical religions in the profound sense that for both religion is 'faith enacted into history,' incapable of being expressed, understood or communicated apart from the history in and through which it is enacted."[40] Reflecting on the festivals of Passover and Easter, Herberg gave eloquent expression to his understanding of the centrality of history to both religious faiths: "We are accustomed to speak of Judaism and Christianity as historical religions in contrast to the non-historical religions and philosophies of Greece and the Far East. That means that Hebraic religion is not a system of abstract propositions but, in the most literal sense, 'a faith enacted as history' and entirely unintelligible and incommunicable apart from that history. There is no Judaism without Abraham and Moses, without Egypt and Sinai; there is no Christianity without these and, in addition, without Jesus and Calvary."[41] Furthermore, argues Herberg, Christianity and Judaism as "historical faiths" must be existentially appropriated or "reenacted" by all believing Jews and Christians,[42] as such believers do during the Easter and Passover festivals: "For the believing Jew and Christian, true to his tradition, these holy days are not mere memorials, like Washington's Birthday or the Fourth of July. They are crucial moments in which eternity enters time, in which the temporal takes on the dimensions of the eternal. They are moments when history is enacted in our own lives."[43]

Moreover, in sharing the view of a "Heilsgeschichte," suggests Herberg, "both Christianity and Judaism share a redemptive history or Sacred Story that moves from 'first things' to 'last things.'" The dramatic moment, he suggested, occurs in three stages: original rightness at creation, the fallen state precipitated by man's sin, and redemption "through repentance and a restoration of the proper relation to God in a total love and obedience."[44] As Bernhard W. Anderson has noted, the difference between Judaism and Christianity for Herberg was "one of vocation during the second act, that is, our present historical existence."[45] For, as Herberg contended, "in the historical drama" the task of the believing Jew is "to stand," to bear faithful witness of God's transcendence in his own existence. The task of the Christian, on the other hand, is "to go out" from Israel and bring the Gentiles into the unfolding drama of God's redemptive purpose. According to this Herbergian view, "Jews and Christians belong to one people, they worship one God, and they share one story; but to each has been given a special vocation."[46] Thus Christians and Jews need each other, for they "stand united until the end of time in the struggle for the Lord of History against the pagan and idolatrous powers that threaten to overwhelm us from every side."[47]

While recognizing the similarities, Herberg did not play down the differences between Christianity and Judaism. While fully realizing that the two faiths differed profoundly on several points, he disagreed with the traditional view that Judaism was a religion of law and works while Christianity was a religion of faith and grace. "The fact of the matter is," he insisted, "that the demand of law and gospel of grace are to be found in both religions; indeed, as Luther once exclaimed, where is the man who can properly distinguish between law and gospel?" Indeed, observed Herberg, it is easy to "misunderstand" and "misrepresent" the alleged difference between the two: "It is not as if law can be assigned to Judaism and grace to Christianity; both affirm law in some sense and both see law transcended and fulfilled in grace and love. Judaism is not salvation by works—the rabbis tell us that 'our father Abraham inherited this world and the world-to-come solely by virtue of his faith'; and the observant Jew prays every morning, 'Our Father, our King, be gracious unto us, for we have no works. Save us according to thy grace.' On the other hand, Christianity does not disregard works—does not Paul himself tell us that 'everyone will be judged according to what he has done, whether it be good or bad' (2 Cor 5:10)?"[48]

The central distinction between the two religions, Herberg insisted, arose over their respective relationship to the covenant, which was "the central category of biblical thinking," and over the answer to the question that Jesus put to his disciples: "Who do you say that I am?" Although, through the covenant, Israel, as God's people, "would be the vehicle whereby all of mankind would be brought under the covenant," this "path to redemption" did not require that all people must embrace Judaism.[49] Rather, for Christians, acceptance of Jesus as the Christ (that is, the messiah) was the point of entry into the sacred covenant established at Sinai, through which Gentiles could become part of the "double covenant" community. Thus, according to Herberg, the meaning that a Jew attributes to Jesus will necessarily differ from that of a Christian: "For the Jew sees Jesus as emerging from Israel and going forth; he sees him from the rear, as it were. The Christian, on the other hand, will see Christ as coming toward him, in the fullness of divine grace, to claim, to judge, and to save; he meets him, as Paul met him on the road to Damascus or as Peter outside Rome, face to face in confrontation."[50]

According to Herberg's understanding of the relationship between Judaism and Christianity, moreover, one of the major differences between the two faiths lay in the differences of mediation between God and man. In Judaism, contended Herberg, one's relationship to God was mediated through the people of Israel, while in Christianity it was through Christ. "This is clearly brought out," he suggests, "in the structure of prayer of the two faiths. Both Christian and Jew open their prayers with an invocation to God, go on to their petitions, and conclude with a kind of commendatory plea. But the Christian says 'through' or 'for the sake of Christ our Lord,' whereas the Jew concludes with 'for the sake of Israel thy people.' The Christian recalls the 'merits of Christ,' while the Jew recalls the 'merits of the fathers' (Abraham, Isaac, and Jacob; i.e., Israel). To be a Jew means to meet and receive his grace in and through Israel; to be a Christian means to meet and receive his grace in and through Christ."[51] Thus, "authentic Judaism" is necessarily "Israel-centered" and oriented to the Sinai-event, while "authentic Christianity" is "Christ-centered" and oriented to Calvary.[52]

And this, Herberg maintains, is the way it should be. The different meanings that Christians and Jews attributed to Jesus should not be explained away or compromised in the name of either theological liberalism or interreligious dialogue. Thus, Herberg insisted that Christians "should take their own messianic faith seriously." Instead of reducing Jesus to the status of a moral teacher or a prophetic voice alone, they should behold him in his splendid uniqueness, as "the God appointed and God incarnate agent through whom the Gentiles are to be brought into the covenant."[53] At the same time, suggests Herberg, the believing Christian should recognize that the "obstinacy" of the believing Jew in "refusing to see in Jesus the fulfillment and completion of God's redemptive work" might be an important and "indispensable reminder of the very incompleteness of this completion, of a redemption which may indeed have come but is nevertheless yet to come." While Christians should recognize that their understanding of Jesus as the messiah will and should continue to mean much more for a believing Christian than it could ever mean for a believing Jew, wrote Herberg, Jews should recognize that such belief in Jesus as messiah is "the way by and through which the peoples of the world may enter the covenant of Israel and come to serve the God of Israel, who is the Creator of the universe and the Lord of all being."[54] While in Jesus, and in the relationship of Jesus to the covenant, Jews and Christians both find that which unites them, and that which separates them, argues Herberg, "the unity far transcends the separation."[55] It is this underlying unity that is the basis for theological understanding and dialogue between both faith communities. For the two, Judaism and Christianity, "are united in their common allegiance to the living and in their common expectation of, and longing for, the One who is to come: for the Christian, the One who came and is to come again, for the Jew the One who is promised to Israel; but for both the same Promised One." In this faith and hope, concludes Herberg, Jew and Christian—to recall Paul

Tillich's words—"stand united until the end of time in the struggle for the Lord of history against the pagan and idolatrous powers that threaten to overwhelm us on every side."[56]

CONCLUSION

Will Herberg deserves to be remembered as an important Jewish theologian of Christianity, as well as a preeminent theologian of Judaism. When Herberg died in 1977, his long-time friend and former Drew University colleague Bernhard Anderson, then dean of the Princeton Theological Seminary, would go so far as to say that "no Christian theologian of the past generation has matched Herberg's ability to interpret and defend the Christian faith. . . . Standing within the Jewish community, Herberg was a vigorous, incisive Christian apologist."[57] His unique ability to understand and interpret Christianity "without surrendering his stance within the Jewish community," suggested Anderson, stemmed from his equally unique ability "to project himself into the Christian faith."[58]

Many Jews, however, felt that as an interpreter and defender of the Christian faith, and as a "vigorous, incisive Christian apologist," Herberg went too far. There is certainly at least some validity to such an assertion. Herberg's ability to "project himself into the Christian faith" found expression, for example, in what Janet Gnall has called his "extraordinary attitude" toward Christmas as a day of homage for Jesus, an attitude shared by few if any other major twentieth century Jewish thinkers. "It seems to me," Herberg wrote, "that whether or not Christmas is a Jewish holiday, it is certainly a holiday of immense significance to believing Jews since it is the day associated with the birth of the figure by way of whom . . . the God of Israel reached the nations of the world. . . . I do not see why we should not join in paying homage to Jesus. We worship none but we owe our homage and reverence to the one who, in divine providence, was chosen from amongst Israel to bring a knowledge of the God of Israel to the peoples of the world."[59] Such a theological understanding of the significance of Christmas is certainly more intrinsic to Christianity than to Judaism, and lends credence to the claim of Herberg's critics that he had more to say to believing Christians than to believing Jews.

Herberg's ability to "project himself into the Christian faith," as if he himself were from within that community, is further evidenced in his published sermon, "The Incarnate Word," which was given during a communion service at Drew University in 1961, at the invitation of the graduating class of the Drew Theological School. A Jewish theologian being invited (and agreeing) to take part in the celebration of the Christian sacrament was an "unprecedented" and controversial event in the Jewish community, and in the Christian community as well. And when Herberg accepted the invitation, it was decided that he would not be an actual officiant in the service, but "would sit in the front pew as an observer, come to the pulpit at the appropriate time for the homily, and return to his seat when he was finished."[60] Nonetheless, his "message" was so authentically Christian that, as one student of Herberg's writing has observed, "many a Jew might shudder at the thought that [his] words were uttered by one who professed to be a believing Jew." Remember, Herberg told his Christian congregation, that

> as you receive the bread and wine in Holy Communion it is the Incarnate Word, fully, really, and truly, that you are receiving—the very same Incarnate Word that died on the cross, was raised on the third day, and was exalted to the right hand of the Father. . . .

> As you receive the Incarnate Word in proclamation and sacrament, in gospel and Holy Communion, you receive once again the new life implanted in you by the grace of God in Christ when he chose you to bring you out of the world into his church. . . . You receive those resources of grace without which your life would be as nothing. . . .

> Remember that the kingship of Christ is not restricted to the visible confines of his church. . . . [T]he communion which you enter into . . . is communion with all men and women everywhere. . . . In Holy Communion, you receive the Incarnate Word of God. God, in his incredible goodness, is making himself available to you in Christ. Realize the immensity of the goodness of God; realize too your own unworthiness and receive God's gracious gift of himself in humility and gratitude. . . .[61]

As one of his Christian colleagues at Drew so aptly noted, the essence of Herberg's communion sermon "was more Christian," even more orthodox Christian, than many communion sermons given by properly ordained Christian ministers.[62] Herberg's Jewish critics would certainly agree. Herberg's Jewishness, like that of Martin Buber's, had always been suspect among traditional Jews because of the absence of a "lived tradition," of a personal commitment to Jewish ritual and observance. For such traditional Jews, already familiar with Herberg's Jewish theology, with his estrangement from the Jewish religious community after the late 1950s,[63] and with his antipathetic views on Zionism and the state of Israel,[64] his very Christian understanding of Christmas and his communion sermon, published in 1976, confirmed their worst suspicion that in his all-too-successful effort to "project himself into the Christian faith," he had become more at home in the church than in the synagogue. Such traditional Jewish readers, who had been put off by Herberg's existentialist approach to Jewish faith generally, and who had found the Jewish theology of *Judaism for Modern Man,* in particular, too intrinsically Christian, felt that as an apologist for the Christian faith, who sought to understand and appreciate Christianity as if he himself were a practicing Christian, Herberg had indeed "surrendered" (or at least compromised) his own Jewish religious identity. Thus, for Herberg's Jewish critics, his understanding of Jesus and Christianity, as well as his interpretation of Jewish theology, has seemed in several crucial respects to be more Christian than Jewish.

NOTES

1. Will Herberg, "From Marxism to Judaism: Jewish Belief as a Dynamic of Social Action," *Commentary,* January 1947, p. 25.

2. Ibid. p. 27.

3. Will Herberg, "Reinhold Niebuhr: Christian Apologist to the Secular World," *Union Seminary Quarterly Review,* May 1956, p. 12.

4. Seymour Siegel, "Will Herberg (1902–1922): A Ba'al Teshuvah Who Became Theologian, Sociologist, Teacher," *American Jewish Year Book,* 1978, p. 532.

5. Ibid.

6. Janet M. Gnall, *Will Herberg, Jewish Theologian: A Biblical Existential Approach to Religion.* Unpublished Ph.D. Dissertation, Drew University, 1983, p. 51.

7. Will Herberg, *Judaism for Modern Man* (New York: Farrar, Straus and Young, 1951), pp. 25–43.

8. Eugene Borowitz, "An Existentialist View of God," *Jewish Heritage,* Spring 1958.

9. Janet Gnall, p. 54.

10. Seymour Siegel, p. 533.

11. Will Herberg, "The Chosenness of Israel and the Jew of Today," *Midstream,* Autumn 1955, p. 88.

12. Herberg, *Judaism and Modern Man*, pp. 244–245.

13. Ibid., p. 246.

14. Will Herberg, "The Theological Problems of the Hour," *Proceedings of the Rabbinical Assembly of America*, June 1949, p. 420.

15. Eugene Borowitz, for example, has pointed out the similarities between Herberg's existentialist view of God and that of the Protestant existentialist Paul Tillich, in "An Existentialist View of God."

16. S. Daniel Breslauer, "Will Herberg: Intuitive Spokesman for American Judaism," *Judaism*, Winter 1978, p. 9.

17. Herberg, "The Theological Problems of the Hour," pp. 424–425.

18. Quoted in Judd L. Teller, "A Critique of the New Jewish Theology," *Commentary*, March 1958, p. 250.

19. Samuel Sandmel has suggested that Herberg "went beyond regarding Niebuhr and Tillich as mentors whose profundity should be emulated, and proceeded to use these men as if they were mentors for Judaism itself." Samuel Sandmel, "Reflections on the Problem of Theology for Jews," *The Journal of Bible and Religion*, April 1956, p. 102.

20. Bernhard W. Anderson, "Will Herberg as Biblical Theologian," in *Faith Enacted into History: Essays in Biblical Theology* (Philadelphia: The Westminster Press, 1976), p. 24.

21. Bernhard W. Anderson, "Herberg as Theologian of Christianity," *National Review*, August 5, 1977, p. 884.

22. Janet Gnall, p. 128.

23. David Novak, *Jewish-Christian Dialogue: A Jewish Justification* (New York: Oxford University Press, 1989), p. 77.

24. For a discussion of the views of some of these Jewish thinkers on Christianity, see Walter Jacob, *Christianity Through Jewish Eyes: The Quest for Common Ground* (Cincinnati: Hebrew Union College Press, 1974), and George L. Berlin, *Defending the Faith: Nineteenth-Century American Jewish Writings on Christianity and Jesus* (Albany: SUNY, 1989).

25. George L. Berlin, ibid., p. 168.

26. Donald Hagner, *The Jewish Reclamation of Jesus: An Analysis and Critique of the Modern Jewish Study of Jesus* (Grand Rapids: Zondervan Publishing House, 1984), p. 13.

27. See, for example, Walter Jacob, op. cit., chapters on Montefiore, Baeck and Klausner; and on Stephen S. Wise: Melvin I. Urofsky, *A Voice That Spoke for Justice: The Life and Times of Stephen S. Wise* (Albany: SUNY Press, 1982), pp. 193–196; and Donald Hagner ibid. pp. 28–31.

28. Martin Buber, *Two Paths of Faith*, trans. N.P. Goldhawk (New York, 1951; rpt. 1963), pp. 12–13.

29. Will Herberg, "A Jew Looks at Jesus," in Bernhard W. Anderson, ed., *Faith Enacted into History*, p. 84.

30. Ibid. p. 85.

31. Ibid.

32. Ibid. pp. 85–86.

33. Will Herberg, "Rosenzweig's 'Judaism of Personal Existence': A Third Way Between Orthodoxy and Modernism," in David G. Dalin, ed., *From Marxism to Judaism: The Collected Essays of Will Herberg* (New York: Markus Wiener Publishing, Inc., 1989), p. 75.

34. Ibid. p. 86.

35. Harry J. Ausmus, *Will Herberg: From Right to Right* (Chapel Hill: The University of North Carolina Press, 1987), p. 122.

36. Will Herberg, "Judaism and Christianity: Their Unity and Difference," in Bernhard W. Anderson, ed., *Faith Enacted Into History*, p. 50.

37. Janet Gnall, op. cit. p. 131.

38. Will Herberg, "A Jew Looks at Jesus," p. 89.

39. Will Herberg, "Judaism and Christianity: Their Unity and Difference," p. 44.

40. Ibid. pp. 45–46.

41. Will Herberg, "Beyond Time and Eternity: Reflections of Passover and Easter," in Bernhard W. Anderson, ed., *Faith Enacted into History*, p. 69.

42. Ibid., and Janet Gnall, p. 137.

43. Will Herberg, "Beyond Time and Eternity: Reflections on Passover and Easter," p. 69.

44. Will Herberg, "Judaism and Christianity: Their Unity and Difference," p. 45.

45. Bernhard W. Anderson, "Herberg as Theologian of Christianity," *National Review,* August 5, 1977, p. 884.

46. Ibid.

47. Ibid.

48. Will Herberg, "Judaism and Christianity: Their Unity and Difference," pp. 55–56.

49. Harry J. Ausmus, p. 122.

50. Will Herberg, "A Jew Looks at Jesus," pp. 90–91.

51. Will Herberg, "Judaism and Christianity: Their Unity and Difference," p. 52.

52. Ibid.; also, for a discussion of this point of Herberg's, see Janet Gnall, pp. 137–138.

53. Bernhard W. Anderson, "Herberg as Theologian of Christianity," p. 884, and Will Herberg, "A Jew Looks at Jesus," p. 89.

54. Will Herberg, "A Jew Looks at Jesus," p. 89.

55. Ibid. p. 93.

56. Ibid.

57. Bernhard W. Anderson, "Herberg as Theologian of Christianity," p. 884.

58. Bernhard W. Anderson, "Will Herberg as Biblical Theologian," in *Faith Enacted into History,* p. 16.

59. Janet Gnall, p. 133.

60. Bernhard W. Anderson, "Will Herberg as Biblical Theologian, p. 16.

61. Bernhard W. Anderson, ed., *Faith Enacted into History: Essays in Biblical Theology,* pp. 95–98.

62. Bernhard W. Anderson, "Will Herberg as Biblical Theologian," p. 16.

63. On this subject, see Seymour Siegel, "Will Herberg: A Ba'al Teshuvah' Who Became Theologian, Sociologist, Teacher," p. 535.

64. On this subject, see David G. Dalin, "Will Herberg in Retrospect," *Commentary,* July 1988, p. 41.

Notes on the Contributors

Dr. S. Daniel Breslauer is Professor of Religious Studies at the University of Kansas. He was ordained at Hebrew Union College and is the author of two books and numerous articles that have appeared in Jewish periodicals.

Rabbi Dr. David Dalin is Associate Professor of American Jewish History at the University of Hartford. A member of the Academic Advisory Council of the American Jewish Historical Society, he is also on the editorial board of *Conservative Judaism* and of *First Things: A Journal of Religion and Public Life*. His book, *From Marxism to Judaism; The Collected Essays of Will Herberg,* was published in 1989. He has contributed numerous articles and book reviews to various periodicals.

Rabbi Dr. Elliot N. Dorff is Provost and Professor of Philosophy at the University of Judaism in Los Angeles. He teaches Jewish law at the law schools of UCLA and the University of Southern California. He is a member of the Conservative Movement's committees on Jewish Law and Standards and on the Philosophy of the Conservative Movement. He also serves on the committee to write a new Torah commentary for Conservative congregations. Dr. Dorff's publications include *Jewish Law and Modern Ideology; Conservative Judaism: Our Ancestors to Our Descendants; A Living Tree: The Roots and Growth of Jewish Law* (with Arthur Rosett); as well as many articles on issues in modern Jewish philosophy and legal theory.

Rabbi Dr. Walter Jacob is Vice President of The Central Conference of American Rabbis. He is the sixteenth generation of rabbis in his family, who served in the United States and Central Europe. He is the author or editor of twelve books, including: *Contemporary American Reform Responsa,* 1987; *Liberal Judaism and Halakhah,* 1988; *Christianity through*

163

Jewish Eyes, 1974; *The Pittsburgh Platform in Retrospect,* 1983; and is the translator and editor of Benno Jacob's *Commentary on Exodus.* He has been rabbi at the Rodef Shalom Congregation since 1955.

Rabbi Leon Klenicki is the Director of the Department of Jewish-Catholic Relations of the Anti-Defamation League of B'nai B'rith and ADL's Liaison to the Vatican.

Dr. David Novak is Edgar M. Bronfman Professor of Modern Judaic Studies at the University of Virginia. He received his Master of Hebrew Literature and rabbinical diploma from the Jewish Theological Seminary of America. He is the author of six books, most recently *Jewish-Christian Dialogue: A Jewish Justification,* as well as numerous articles. Dr. Novak serves as Vice President of the Institute on Religion and Public Life and is on the editorial board of its journal, *First Things.* His professional affiliations include the Association for Jewish Studies, the American Academy of Religion, the Jewish Law Association, the American Theological Society and the Academy for Jewish Philosophy, where he is Director of Publications.

Rabbi Dr. Norman Solomon is Director of the Centre for the Study of Judaism and Jewish/Christian Relations at Selly Oak Colleges, Birmingham, England.

Dr. Michael Wyschogrod is Professor of Philosophy at Baruch College of the City University of New York, and former Director of the Institute for Jewish-Christian Relations of the American Jewish Congress. He is the author, most recently, of *The Body of Faith: God and the People Israel.* He has also contributed many articles to American and European periodicals.

Index

Abba Ben Kahana, 125
Abbahu, Rav, 121, 122–23, 135
Abraham, 3, 18, 19, 134
Accommodationist theology, 89–90, 93
Achan, 20
Acts, Book of, 133–34
Agus, Jacob Bernard, 18, 128
Akiba, Rabbi, 48, 51–52, 124
Albo, Isaac, 5
Albo, Joseph, 51
Amos, 134
Anderson, Bernhard W., 150, 154, 157
Anglican-Jewish Consultation, 1987, 36
Antiochus IV, 7
Antisemitism, 4, 32–33, 109, 134
Anti-Zionism, 32–33
Aristotle, 90
Asch, Shalom, 69
Augustine, 23, 33–34
Auschwitz. *See* Holocaust
Ayer, A. J., 53

Bachya Ibn Pakuda, 127–28, 129
Baeck, Leo, 69–71, 75, 76, 78, 81, 82, 151
Balaam, 125–26
Barth, Karl, 150
Benamozegh, Elijah, 10, 68, 78
Bible, 18–19, 58–59, 129–30; New Testament, 4, 9, 30, 83, 123, 126
Billerbeck, Paul, 77, 78
Boniface, Count, 34
Borowitz, Eugene, 67, 82, 120
Braithwaite, R. B., 53
Breslauer, S. Daniel, 149

Brod, Max, 74
Buber, Martin, 1, 75–76, 79, 81, 128, 137–38; relating to Christians, 13–15; covenant, 47; Herberg and, 146, 147, 150, 151, 152, 158
Bunam, Simhah, Rabbi, 128

Catholics. *See* Roman Catholics
Christ. *See* Jesus Christ
Church of England, 38
Clement of Alexandria, 23
Cohen, Arthur A., 136
Cohen, Gerson D., 146
Cohen, Hermann, 69, 73, 143
Commentary, 146
Conservative Jews, 49
Constantine, 9
Contemporary Christologies: A Jewish Response (Borowitz), 67, 82
Covenant, 6, 9, 17–22, 43–66, 78, 81, 91, 127; God, role of, 62–63; group, role of, 61; Hebrew scriptures and, 18–19; individuals, role of, 60–62; Jewish ambivalence about, 43–44; nationality and, 20; rabbis and, 19–20, 45; Sinai covenant, 9, 20, 46, 58, 99; universal ideals, role of 61–62
Creation, 96–97

Daniel (Buber), 14
Declaration on Religious Liberty, 57
Diogenes Laertius, 21
Disputations, 5, 87–91
Donatists, 34

165

other volumes in this series

Stepping Stones to Further Jewish-Christian Relations: An Unabridged Collection of Christian Documents, compiled by Helga Croner (A Stimulus Book, 1977).

Helga Croner and Leon Klenicki, editors, *Issues in the Jewish-Christian Dialogue: Jewish Perspectives on Covenant, Mission and Witness* (A Stimulus Book, 1979).

Clemens Thoma, *A Christian Theology of Judaism* (A Stimulus Book, 1980).

Helga Croner, Leon Klenicki and Lawrence Boadt, C.S.P., editors, *Biblical Studies: Meeting Ground of Jews and Christians* (A Stimulus Book, 1980).

John T. Pawlikowski, O.S.M., *Christ in the Light of the Christian-Jewish Dialogue* (A Stimulus Book, 1982)

Martin Cohen and Helga Croner, editors, *Christian Mission-Jewish Mission* (A Stimulus Book, 1982).

Leon Klenicki and Gabe Huck, editors, *Spirituality and Prayer: Jewish and Christian Understandings* (A Stimulus Book, 1983).

Leon Klenicki and Geoffrey Wigoder, editors, *A Dictionary of the Jewish-Christian Dialogue* (A Stimulus Book, 1984).

Edward Flannery, *The Anguish of the Jews* (A Stimulus Book, 1985).

More Stepping Stones to Jewish-Christian Relations: An Unabridged Collection of Christian Documents 1975–1983, compiled by Helga Croner (A Stimulus Book, 1985).

Clemens Thoma and Michael Wyschogrod, editors, *Understanding Scripture: Explorations of Jewish and Christian Traditions of Interpretation* (A Stimulus Book, 1987).

Bernard J. Lee, S. M., *The Galilean Jewishness of Jesus* (A Stimulus Book, 1988).

Clemens Thoma and Michael Wyschogrod, editors, *Parable and Story in Judaism and Christianity* (A Stimulus Book, 1989).

Eugene J. Fisher and Leon Klenicki, editors, *In Our Time: The Flowering of Jewish-Catholic Dialogue* (A Stimulus Book, 1990).

STIMULUS BOOKS are developed by Stimulus Foundation, a not-for-profit organization, and are published by Paulist Press. The Foundation wishes to further the publication of scholarly books on Jewish and Christian topics that are of importance to Judaism and Christianity.

Stimulus Foundation was established by an erstwhile refugee from Nazi Germany who intends to contribute with these publications to the improvement of communication between Jews and Christians.

Books for publication in this Series will be selected by a committee of the Foundation, and offers of manuscripts and works in progress should be addressed to:

Stimulus Foundation
785 West End Ave.
New York, N.Y. 10025